DNA and BODY EVIDENCE

FORENSIC EVIDENCE

DNA and BODY EVIDENCE

BRIAN INNES

SERIES CONSULTANT: RONALD L. SINGER, M.S.
PRESIDENT, INTERNATIONAL ASSOCIATION OF FORENSIC SCIENCES

Sharpe Focus

an imprint of M.E. Sharpe, Inc.

First edition for the United States, its territories and dependencies,
Canada, Mexico, and Australia, published in 2008 by M.E. Sharpe, Inc.

Sharpe Focus
An imprint of M.E. Sharpe, Inc.
80 Business Park Drive
Armonk, NY 10504

www.mesharpe.com

ISBN: 978-0-7656-8115-7

Library of Congress Cataloging-in-Publication Data

Innes, Brian.
  DNA and body evidence / Brian Innes.
     p. cm. -- (Forensic evidence)
  Includes bibliographical references and index.
  ISBN 978-0-7656-8115-7 (hardcover : alk. paper)
  1. DNA fingerprinting--Juvenile literature. 2. DNA--Analysis--Juvenile
literature. 3. Forensic genetics--Juvenile literature. 4. Criminal
investigation--Juvenile literature. I. Title.

RA1057.55.I565 2008
614'.1--dc22
                          2007006749

Editorial and design by Amber Books Ltd
Project Editor: Michael Spilling
Copy Editor: Brian Burns
Picture Research: Kate Green
Design: Richard Mason

Cover Design: Jesse Sanchez, M.E. Sharpe, Inc.

Printed in Malaysia

9 8 7 6 5 4 3 2 1

Contents

Introduction

As we approach the end of the first decade of the twenty-first century, interest in the forensic sciences continues to grow. The continued popularity of television shows such as *CSI, Crossing Jordan, Bones*, and the like has stimulated such an interest in forensic science among middle and high-school students that many schools now offer "forensic science" as a subject choice alongside the more traditional subjects of biology, chemistry, and physics. Each year, the number of colleges and universities offering majors in forensic science at both undergraduate and graduate level has increased, and more and more graduates are entering the job market looking for positions in the forensic science industry. The various disciplines that comprise forensic science provide the opportunity to use education and training in ways that the average student may imagine is rarely possible. On a day-to-day basis, the forensic scientist is called upon to apply the laws of science to the solution of problems that may link a particular individual to a particular crime scene or incident. Alternatively, the same tools and techniques may exonerate an innocent person who has been wrongly accused of committing a crime.

The four books that make up this series—*DNA and Body Evidence, Fingerprints and Impressions, Fire and Explosives*, and *Hair and Fibers*—are designed to introduce the reader to the various disciplines that comprise the forensic sciences. Each is devoted to a particular specialty, describing in depth the actual day-to-day activities of the expert. The volumes also describe the science behind those activities, and the education and training required to perform those duties successfully. Every aspect of forensic science and forensic investigation is covered, including DNA fingerprinting, crime scene investigation and procedure, detecting trace evidence, fingerprint analysis, shoe and boot prints, fabric prints, ear prints, blood sampling, arson investigation, explosives

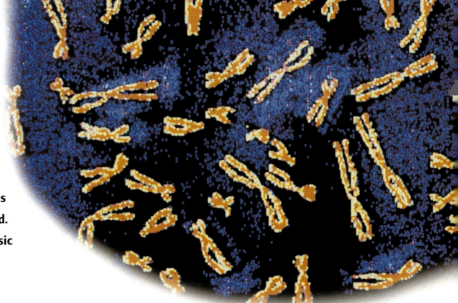

Under the microscope, this colored-light micrograph shows how the forty-six chromosomes of a human cell are paired. The chromsome is the basic building block of human genetic makeup.

analysis, laboratory testing, and the use of forensic evidence in the courtroom, to cover just a brief sample of what the four volumes of *Forensic Evidence* have to offer. Pull-out feature boxes focus on important aspects of forensic equipment, procedures, key facts, and important case studies.

Numerous criminal cases are described to demonstrate the uses and limits of forensic investigation, including such famous and landmark cases as the O.J. Simpson trial; cases of mistaken identity, such as Will West, who was at first confused with his identical twin and eventually cleared via fingerprint analysis; and the work of the Innocence Project, which has used DNA analysis to retrospectively overturn wrongful convictions.

In *DNA and Body Evidence*, the author covers the history and use of body fluids and blood in forensic investigation, genetic analysis, DNA fingerprinting, gathering trace evidence at the crime scene, famous cases—such as notorious serial killer Jack Unterweger, who was eventually convicted using DNA analysis from a single hair—and the admissibility of DNA evidence in the courtroom. Written in a plain, accessible style, the series is aimed squarely at the general reader with an interest in forensic science and crime scene analysis, and does not assume previous knowledge of the subject. All technical language is either explained in the text, or covered in an easy-to-reference glossary on pages 92–93.

Taken as a whole, the *Forensic Evidence* series serves as a comprehensive resource in a highly readable format.

Ronald L. Singer, M.S.
President, International Association of Forensic Sciences

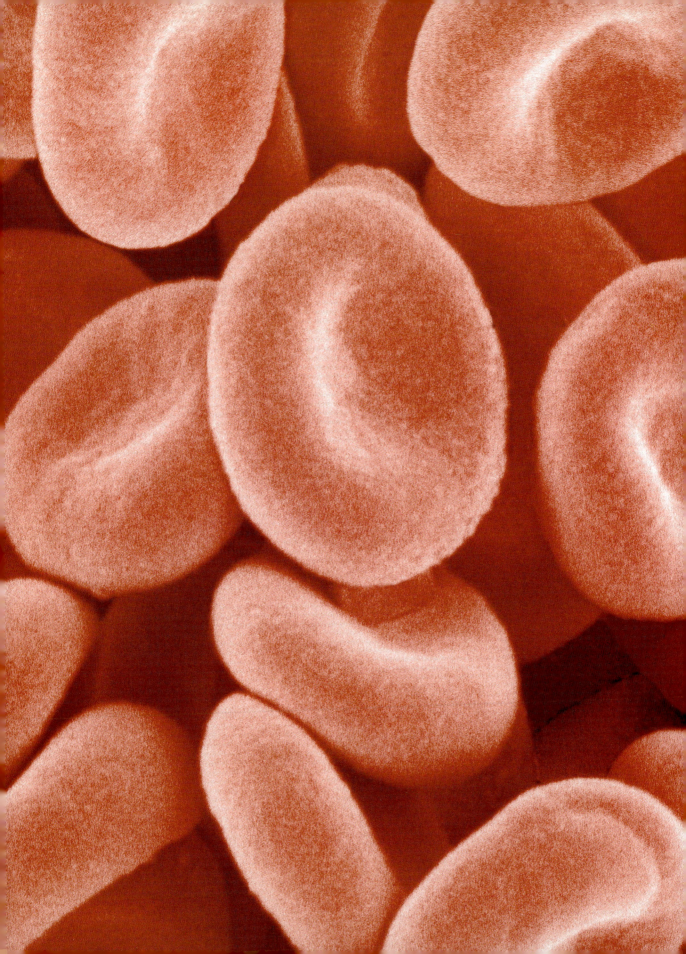

chapter 1

Blood Evidence

All body fluids—especially blood—contain specific substances that provide essential clues in the investigation of crime.

Blood is the most essential part of the human body. Pumped by the heart, it carries oxygen from the lungs to the tissues, together with nutrients and many of the chemicals needed to provide energy and keep the body functioning. For the forensic scientist, blood also plays an important part in the investigation of many types of crimes.

In many crimes of violence, the most obvious evidence is blood. It was not until last century, however, that forensic investigators were able to develop techniques of analyzing this evidence. First, they found methods to distinguish one type of blood from another. Then they looked at what the splashes of blood could reveal about the circumstances of the crime. But over the past twenty years all the body fluids—and not just blood—have provided vital evidence in the investigation of every type of crime. This is because the analysis of the substance **deoxyribonucleic** (*dee-oxy-ry-bo-nu-kle-ik*)

◁ **The red cells—called erythrocytes—give blood its distinctive color. They are the only cells in the human body that have no nucleus, and so do not contain DNA. They are, however, the means by which oxygen is carried to all the tissues.**

acid (DNA), which can be found in most human cells, can detect a single individual among the total population of the world.

Understanding Blood

For many centuries, **anatomists** puzzled over what blood actually did. In 1616, the English physician William Harvey established the connection between the beating of the heart and the circulation of blood through the body. Not long after that, physicians began to wonder whether it was possible to give blood to someone dying from loss of blood, or to someone suffering from anemia (lack of red blood cells).

In 1650, Christopher Wren (later the architect of St. Paul's Cathedral, and many other churches, in London) invented the first hypodermic syringe (an instrument designed for injecting substances into the blood). It was a sharpened, slender goose quill, with a bladder attached to the other end.

At this time, physicians believed that all blood was the same, whatever its source. In 1668, Dr. Jean Denys, of

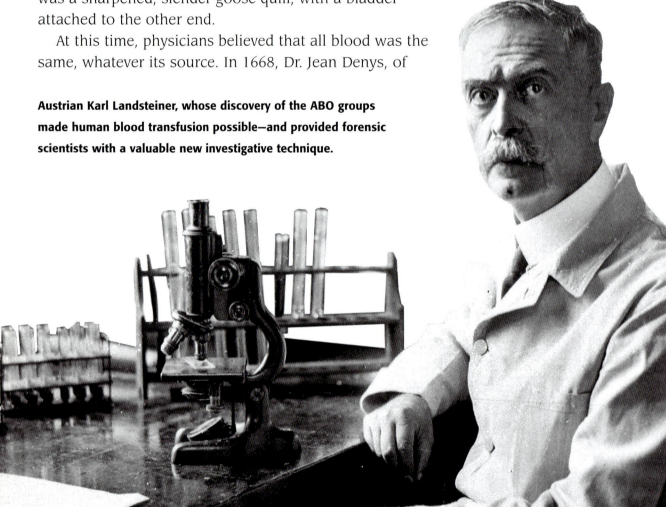

Austrian Karl Landsteiner, whose discovery of the ABO groups made human blood transfusion possible—and provided forensic scientists with a valuable new investigative technique.

Montpellier, France, attempted to treat one of his patients with sheep's blood. The patient died, and Denys was ordered to stop his experiments immediately. In England in 1814, Dr. James Blundell successfully gave one dog another dog's blood, but when he used sheep's blood the dog died almost immediately. Four years later, Blundell tried transfusing human blood. Some of his patients survived, but others died. It became obvious that not all blood was the same, and for many years physicians considered blood transfusion too dangerous to attempt.

The Cause Discovered

In 1875, the German **physiologist** Leonard Landois took the red blood cells from one animal and mixed them with the serum (the clear liquid of the blood) from a different species. The red cells immediately clumped together. Landois thought this might explain why attempts at blood transfusion were unsuccessful, but it was some time before the real reason was discovered.

Karl Landsteiner, an assistant professor at the Institute of Pathology in Vienna, Austria, followed up on Landois's experiments. In 1900, he discovered different types of blood and that mixing two types together caused **agglutination**. At first, he identified three types, which he named A, B, and C. Later, because it was the commonest type of human blood, C was renamed O. Soon afterward, one of Landsteiner's colleagues discovered a fourth type. It did not agglutinate either A or B, and was named AB.

The red blood cells of types A, B, and AB carry antigens—substances that help to produce antibodies that fight infection. When two incompatible antigens come together, they cause agglutination. In 1909, Landsteiner classified the four blood groups as follows:

- Group A: antigen A present, antigen B absent
- Group B: antigen B present, antigen A absent
- Group O: both antigens absent
- Group AB: both antigens present

In a blood transfusion, it is possible to give a person with type A blood from another person with type A or type O—because, naturally, group A is a perfect

CASE STUDY THE MAD CARPENTER

On July 2, 1901, police discovered the scattered remains of two young brothers in woodland on the island of Rügen, off the Baltic coast in Germany. Wandering carpenter Ludwig Tessnow, who was not one of the local farming community, was the principal suspect. Investigators found dark stains on his boots and clothing. He protested his innocence, claiming that the stains were wood dye. However, the examining magistrate remembered reading a newspaper report of a similar case several hundred miles away, in Osnabrück. Two young girls had been killed in much the same way, and Tessnow had been one of those questioned at the time.

Three weeks before the Rügen murders, a farmer had found seven of his sheep hacked to pieces and saw a man running from the meadow. The farmer identified that man as Tessnow. The magistrate, who had read reports of the tests developed by Paul Uhlenhuth to distinguish human blood from animal blood, now ordered investigators to send Tessnow's clothes to Uhlenhuth. After several weeks of painstaking tests, Uhlenhuth told the magistrate that some of the stains were sheep's blood, and others were human. Tessnow was found guilty of murder and executed.

match and type O does not have either antigen, so there will be no agglutination.

A person with type B can be given blood of type B or O—again, because B is a perfect match and O does not have either antigen.

A person with type AB can be given blood of any type—because it contains both antigens.

A person with type O, however, can be given only O blood—because it does not have either antigen, so any of the other blood types would cause agglutination.

This discovery opened the way for the millions of successful blood transfusions that have saved many lives.

The proportions of each blood group vary from one national population to another. In the United States, for example, the proportions are approximately as follows:

- Group A: 39 percent
- Group B: 13 percent
- Group O: 43 percent
- Group AB: 5 percent

Blood Inheritance

Landsteiner recognized that people inherited their blood type from their parents. He was the first person to suggest using blood group testing as a way of determining who a person's parents were. He did not imagine, however, how important the technique would soon become in forensic investigation. If, for example, a victim of assault or murder is type O, and bloodstains of this type are found on the clothing of a suspect whose type is A, there is a strong suspicion that these have come from the victim.

German biologist Paul Uhlenhuth developed a simple test to distinguish human from animal blood, and also identify different animal species. He had his first forensic success within months, in the case of Ludwig Tessnow, the "Mad Carpenter."

At the same time, the Belgian physiologist Jules Bordet, working at the Pasteur Institute in Paris, France, had discovered that if he injected a laboratory animal with milk or egg white, it developed a specific antibody against this material. When he then mixed the animal's blood serum with milk or egg white, it produced a cloudy substance, which he called **precipitin**.

In 1901, the German biologist Paul Uhlenhuth followed up on Bordet's discovery and developed a test to distinguish human blood from the blood of other animals. At the same time, this gave him a way to identify many different animal species, using a wide range of serums. Within months, he was able to apply the technique to a murder case.

Blood Tests

Simple ABO typing is of limited value in forensic investigation, although it has provided important circumstantial evidence in many cases.

However, as Landsteiner predicted, ABO typing has proved particularly useful in paternity claims because A and B are dominant over O. Therefore:

- If one parent is type A and the other type O, the child's blood type will be A
- If one parent is type B, and the other O, the child's blood type will be B
- If both parents are type O, the child's blood type will be O
- If both parents have type AB, they can never have a child with blood type O
- Parents of types AO and BO could produce an O child, an A or B child, or an AB child

With this information, and a knowledge of the proportion of each blood type in the population, analysts—known as **serologists**—can almost certainly determine who a child's parents are, or establish someone's ancestry.

Enzymes

Blood also contains many enzymes—protein substances that can cause chemical reactions, without themselves changing. They are essential to the body's energy levels and functioning. Researchers have now discovered that different blood types have different **proteins** and enzymes.

In forensic laboratories, scientists use a technique called **electrophoresis** to separate and identify specific enzymes and proteins in a blood sample. They soak a short piece of thread in the blood and embed it in a thin gel on a plate of glass. Because they use a short piece of thread, they can also lay a number of comparison samples along the length of the plate and treat them at the same time. They then pass a direct electric current through the gel, which makes the protein and enzyme **molecules** move from one side of the plate to the other. Each kind of molecule is of a different size and moves at a different speed, so the different molecules separate. After a set time, the separated molecules are revealed. The scientists then stain them with chemical dyes to identify them. The plate is then photographed.

Unfortunately, heat, sunlight, and other factors cause blood samples to deteriorate rapidly, so evidence samples must be frozen as soon as possible.

Male and Female Blood

In 1949, two British scientists made another important discovery that has proved very useful to criminal investigators. They found that it was possible

KEY FACTS **SECRETORS**

In 1925, scientists made another important discovery. About 80 percent of the population are secretors. Their sweat, urine, saliva, and other body fluids contain the same antigens as their blood. Therefore, even if investigators do not find blood at a crime scene, other traces can help to identify the perpetrator. Evidence of this kind has proved particularly important in cases of physical assault.

Every scrap of evidence gathered at a crime scene, like this household hammer, must be carefully examined for traces of blood and other body fluids.

KEY FACTS **WORKING WITH STATISTICS**

Serologists now have a good idea how often specific enzymes occur in sections of the population, and this is a great help in identification. For example, in the United States 43 percent of the population have blood type O. Of this 43 percent, 36 percent have a substance called haptoglobin-2 (Hp-2) in their blood, and just 5 percent have an enzyme called PGM-2. The probability that one person will have blood type O containing both Hp-2 and PGM-2 is 7,740 in one million. In other words, approximately eight persons in every 1,000 will have this specific blood type.

This is, of course, insufficient evidence in itself, but forensic investigators need only to detect one more protein substance in a blood sample to narrow down the probability to a single suspect.

Many white blood cells (leukocytes) contain granules that can be colored purple with a dye. Adult human blood contains up to 10,000 per cubic millimeter.

to distinguish between male and female body cells, particularly the white blood cells (leukocytes—*lew-ko-sites*) and the cells of the lining of the mouth. The **nucleus** of a female cell contains a body called the Barr body (after one of its discoverers). The Barr body does not occur in male cells and can be stained using chemical dyes.

The science of serology has now been developed to the point where scientists can carry out a series of complex tests on a blood sample in just a few minutes.

Is it Blood?

When investigators discover stains that look like bloodstains, the first thing they have to do is determine whether these are, in fact, blood or not. At a crime scene, investigators take a sample of the stain using a moistened cotton-bud, and transfer it to a paper test strip. The strip contains a chemical that turns blue-green in the presence of blood.

Indoors, murderers often try to wash walls and floors clean. However, blood traces always remain, even if they are not visible to the naked eye. Investigators can reveal these traces by spraying suspected areas with a fluorescent chemical, and then illuminating the areas with ultraviolet light in the dark. The traces glow brightly, revealing spots, splashes, drag marks, and bloody footprints and handprints.

The commonest chemicals used are luminol and fluorescein. Luminol can reveal traces of blood as little as one part in 10 million. It can even reveal traces in cases where criminals have painted the walls.

In the laboratory, the standard test procedure is known as the Kastle-Meyer test. Investigators extract some of the suspect stain using a damp filter paper, and treat it with a mixture of **phenolphthalein** and **hydrogen peroxide**. If it turns pink, it indicates the presence of the blood enzyme peroxidase. There is, however, a drawback: certain vegetables such as potato and horseradish also contain peroxidase—although it would be very unusual to find traces of these vegetables in association with blood. There are two other tests for confirmation: the Teichmann and Takayama tests, named after their respective rsearchers. Both tests involve reactions between a chemical and the **hemoglobin** of red blood cells (erythrocytes), causing crystals to form that can be seen under a microscope.

The next question investigators ask is: is this human blood? In Britain, in 1978, a goat was discovered chewing on an old jacket. There was a hole in the left breast, surrounded by what looked like powder burns from a gunshot, and some blood. A major murder hunt began, with the police searching for a victim. However, when the forensic laboratory made its report, the authorities called off

CASE STUDY   NAMING A MURDERER

On October 23, 1983, the wealthy Laitner family, who lived in a suburb of Sheffield, England, celebrated the wedding of their eldest daughter and then went to bed. Some time during the night, a knife-wielding maniac entered the home. He killed lawyer Basil Laitner, his wife Avril, and their son Richard, and assaulted their daughter, Nichole.

Before carrying out the attack, the man had injured his leg, and so left a bloody print in Nichole's bedroom. Investigators sent the evidence to the Home Office forensic laboratory, where forensic scientists discovered that the blood sample contained a combination of blood factors likely to be found in only one in 50,000 people. Remarkably, the sample matched the blood taken from a suspect and analyzed only a month before. Police had arrested Arthur Hutchinson, a thief, age forty-two, on a charge of rape on September 28. He escaped from the police station by jumping from a high bathroom window, injuring his leg. He was finally captured as he made his way to a hospital for treatment.

the investigation. The hole, the laboratory concluded, was caused by an acid, probably from a car battery. The acid had reacted with the dyes in the fabric to produce the black and red-brown stains.

The method used to identify human blood is a modern development of Uhlenhuth's precipitin test. Investigators place a few drops of a blood sample in one depression in a glass slide that has been coated with gel (as in electrophoresis). They place a specific serum in another depression immediately next to the first one. They then pass a direct electric current through the gel, which causes the two samples to move toward one another. A visible line of precipitin forms where they meet. The method is so sensitive that investigators have even obtained positive results from dried blood traces more than fifteen years old. Successful tests have also been carried out on tissue samples from ancient mummies.

An analyst carries out the phenolphthalein test on two evidence samples. A mixture with hydrogen peroxide will turn pink in the presence of blood.

The star shape of these splashes of blood reveals that they fell vertically from someone standing around the spot.

Investigators still use ABO typing, and the other serological tests outlined in this chapter, because they are quick and positive. However, most forensic analysis of blood and other body liquids are now devoted to the investigation of DNA (*see* Chapter 2).

Blood Spatter

The adult human body contains more than 10 pints (4.7 liters) of blood. Violent crimes almost always leave bloody traces at the scene. If there has been a struggle, some may be the attacker's blood, and every spot must be examined— first by ABO typing—in case it can be sent for DNA analysis. However, the victim's blood is likely to be mixed with the attacker's, which may make DNA analysis difficult.

In most cases, the victim is present at the scene, and blood analysis is necessary only if the identity is unknown. Details of the pattern of blood traces, however, reveal a great deal about the nature of the attack.

Knife stabs and slashes usually produce a lot of blood. If an artery is severed, the pumping action of the heart sends spurts of blood a remarkable distance. A cut vein, however, floods only the surrounding area. Murderers sometimes slash their victim's body after death to try to hide the true cause of death. A dead body, however, does not bleed like a living person—the blood only oozes out.

Attacks with a blunt instrument—a baseball bat, a pistol butt, or even a brick—can also produce blood, and if the assailant swings the weapon several times, splashes of blood from the first wound are thrown behind and above him. Repeated frenzied slashing or stabbing causes the same effect.

Telltale Blood Traces

In 1984, evidence of blood spatter played a vital part in the arrest of Graham Backhouse. He had told the police that his life was under threat and that someone had destroyed his wife's car with a pipe bomb. He agreed to have an alarm installed at his home, linked to the local police station.

KEY FACTS **TYPES OF BLOOD SPATTER**

Blood spatter has been classified into six main types:

- **Drops** are found on horizontal surfaces. They are roughly circular in shape, depending on what height they have fallen from. The greater the height, the more likely that the impact will cause them to spray out in a star shape.
- **Splashes** can be found on sloping surfaces or, more importantly, when the victim has been bludgeoned several times. The splash is shaped like an exclamation mark or a tadpole. The head indicates the direction the blood was traveling, and therefore the direction it came from.
- **Spurts** of blood from an artery can reach the walls and ceiling, and frequently stain the clothing of the attacker—which is very important if a suspect is later arrested.
- **Pools** of blood form around a dying victim. They can indicate that he has dragged himself from one place to another, or been carried there.
- **Smears** on the floor or walls may be left by the victim as she attempts to move while dying, or by the bloodstained attacker.
- **Trails** indicate that a bloody corpse has been moved. If it is dragged, it leaves a smeared trail; if carried, it leaves drops of blood along the way.

Finally, a clear area surrounded by blood spatter indicates that something stood there during the attack, and has since been taken away.

Graham Backhouse, with one of the knife slashes he claimed had been inflicted by his neighbor. But examination of his kitchen floor showed that he had deliberately wounded himself.

On the evening of April 30, 1984, the alarm sounded. When the police arrived, they found Backhouse standing in the kitchen, covered in blood from deep slashes across his face and chest. A shotgun lay beside him and the body of his neighbor Colyn Bedale-Taylor was at the foot of the stairs, shot at point-blank range in the chest, with a craft knife in his hand. Backhouse said that Bedale-Taylor had attacked him in the kitchen, and that he had shot him in self-defense.

When a forensic expert examined the scene, he observed that the blood drops on the kitchen floor were round, indicating that Backhouse had been standing still as he bled. If there had been a struggle like the one he described, the blood would have been flung about in the characteristic exclamation mark shape.

Also, kitchen chairs had fallen on top of some of the round spots, and one had smears of Backhouse's blood along its top—but there was no blood on his gun. Although Bedale-Taylor's body was at the far end of the passage leading from the kitchen, there was no trail of blood. This indicated that Backhouse had staged the scene, and inflicted the wounds on himself, after shooting his victim. It turned out that both men had been locked in a dispute.

At trial, a **pathologist** testifying for the prosecution stated: "The wounds could have been caused by someone else, but Backhouse would have had to stand there doing nothing, while his attacker slashed him from shoulder to hip." The killer was sentenced to two terms of life imprisonment.

Attack on a Widow

Elderly widow Ellen Anderson was the victim of a serious attack in Oregon, during the 1970s. She was severely beaten, but fortunately she survived and was able to testify at trial. She named her assailant as Leslie Harley, a young woman who helped with housework, ran errands, and in fact acted as an unpaid companion. Anderson claimed that, when Harley learned that she was not named in the widow's will, she picked up a poker from the fireplace and struck her in a rage. Then she struck again and again, pursuing her into the living room, up the stairs, and into the bedroom, where she collapsed onto the bed. Blood spatter was found in all these places, including on the bedroom ceiling.

In her defense, Harley claimed that Anderson had fallen and hit her head on the fireplace. She also claimed that she had helped the widow to her bedroom, and offered to telephone a doctor from a list on the bedside table. Harley insisted that the blood on the ceiling came from the widow shaking her head as she suggested each doctor's name.

Dr. Herbert MacDonnell, an expert on blood spatter, acting on behalf of the prosecution, was certain that the blood on the bedroom ceiling could not have come from Anderson's shaking head—even if she had done it with such violence that they reached that high. From their angle of impact, MacDonnell was certain that the stains could have been caused only by Harley repeatedly swinging the poker at the widow's head and body.

To make his testimony convincing to a trial jury, MacDonnell provided a practical example on film. He found a long-haired young nurse, who volunteered to play the part of the victim, with her hair soaked in pig blood. No matter how vigorously she shook her head, no drops reached the ceiling. To prove it beyond all doubt, MacDonnell took a short broom handle dipped in blood, and struck again and again at a pillow placed on a table. The blood pattern on the ceiling was very similar to the blood pattern found in the widow's bedroom. Harley was found guilty of the attack.

It was at this point in the study of blood evidence that a new, and extremely valuable, technique first began to excite forensic scientists. This new technique was the way in which the DNA of an individual person could be characterized.

This Jacksonville, Arkansas, police officer knows that a trail of liquid blood can provide valuable evidence in a street crime.

chapter 2

Genetic Traces

The story of how DNA was discovered and analyzed is a fascinating one. Every individual's is different, and laboratory analysis can lead to a positive identification.

At a crime scene, a criminal can leave behind traces of DNA in a number of ways—for example, in traces of blood, saliva, or semen, and in strands of hair or pieces of skin. Investigators can match DNA samples from the scene to a suspect's DNA and positively identify the perpetrator—just as they can with a unique fingerprint. To understand how, it is first necessary to understand what DNA is and what it does— an understanding that has been building, gradually, for more than a century. Inside every cell of the human body—and inside every body cell of every animal species too—there is a nucleus. The nucleus is, in fact, the largest part inside the cell, and it is vital in controlling most of the body's **metabolism** (met-ab-ol-ism).

In 1879, German biologist Walther Flemming observed, under a high-power microscope, that the nucleus contained

◁ **A police forensic scientist using a tiny swab to take a sample of blood spatter from the license plate of a car, following a street shooting incident. It is essential to establish that this is the blood of the victim, and not the assailant's.**

tiny threadlike structures, paired together. Because these structures easily absorbed the dyes used to stain cells—to make their structure visible—they were named **chromosomes** (*kro-mo-somes*), from the Greek for "color" and "body." The nucleus of human cells contains twenty-three pairs of chromosomes. Flemming noticed that the pairs of chromosomes split up and then became copied and shared between both cells.

Soon after, another German biologist, August Weismann, suggested that it was because of chromosomes that we inherit from our mother and father characteristics such as build, color of hair, skin, and eyes, and many other aspects of the body that cannot even be seen. This is known as **heredity**. Weismann suggested that a specific chemical was responsible for heredity, but at that time he had no idea what it was.

Meanwhile, a Swiss biochemist, Friedrich Miescher, was working with white blood cells or leucocytes (*see* Chapter 1, page 16) to identify the chemical composition of cells. Miescher eventually isolated a chemical from the cell nucleus. One of his students named the chemical **nucleic acid**.

By the end of the nineteenth century, scientists had identified the building blocks of nucleic acid as:

The painstaking work of American biologist Oswald Avery, over a period of 14 years, laid the foundations of modern genetic research. His investigations were an important step in the search for the structure of DNA.

- a simple plant sugar called **ribose** (*ry-bose*)
- a molecular group containing **phosphorus** (*foss-for-us*)
- a set of five compounds containing nitrogen, known as **purine bases**, called:
    - adenine (A)
    - cytosine (C)
    - guanine (G)
    - thymine (T)
    - uracil (U)

Later, it was found that each ribose had one of these purine bases sticking out from the side. The complete molecule was named ribonucleic (*ry-bo-nu-kle-ik*) acid (**RNA**). It was a long time, however, before scientists were able to prove that nucleic acid controlled heredity.

In 1904, Thomas Hunt Morgan became professor of zoology at Columbia University. From his work with the cells of the tiny fruit fly *Drosophila*, which had only four chromosomes, Morgan concluded that hereditary characteristics were indeed passed from one generation to the next by structures strung like beads along the threadlike chromosomes. He called these structures genes.

Then, in the 1920s, analysts discovered that there were two kinds of nucleic acid. The newly discovered nucleic acid contained less oxygen than RNA, so scientists called it deoxyribonucleic (*dee-oxy-ry-bo-nu-kle-ik*) acid—or DNA, for short. RNA contains the purine bases A, C, G, and U. DNA contains the purine bases A, C, G, and T.

Researching DNA

From 1930 through 1944, American microbiologist Oswald Avery and his research team carried out a program of experiments with bacteria. They found that they could change the hereditary characteristics of a growing colony of bacteria by adding dead bacteria of another, similar type. They discovered that DNA was being transferred from one colony to the other. It was therefore clear that DNA contained the genes—the structures that Morgan had identified as responsible for passing on hereditary characteristics. However, it also became clear that the structure of DNA could not be the same for all individuals, because

A model of a short length of DNA. Each of the molecules that make up the complex twisted "ladder" is colored according to its particular type. Altogether, there are some three billion units in the complete chain.

one person's genes had to be different from another's. Otherwise, everyone would be identical. DNA therefore had to have many different internal structures. The hunt was now on to discover the structure of the DNA molecule. In 1950, Austrian-born Erwin Chargaff, working at Columbia University, published a set of rules stating that:

- the total quantity of A+G in any sample of DNA is equal to C+T
- the quantity of A is equal to the quantity of T
- the quantity of G is equal to the quantity of C

DNA Helixes

Two years earlier, in 1948, Linus Pauling had been a visiting lecturer at Oxford University, England. He was researching the structure of proteins, as was Lawrence Bragg at the Cavendish Laboratory in Cambridge, England. Independently, and at almost the same time, both men showed that proteins are coiled **helixes**. It seemed likely that DNA would be similar in shape. However, two of Bragg's young colleagues, American James Watson and Englishman Francis Crick, thought that DNA would have a more complicated structure. They began to build models of double-helix-shaped coils, joined together by bridges of A-T and C-G—like a long, tightly twisted ladder. In 1953, Rosalind Franklin, working at King's College in London, confirmed this structure using x-ray crystallography photographs (*see* X-ray Crystallography, page 31). The sides of DNA's long, tightly twisted ladder are made up of alternating molecules of deoxyribose (S) and the phosphorus compound (P). The rungs of the ladder are composed of two purine bases, linked at each side to an S molecule. Base A on one side of the ladder is always opposite and linked to base T on the opposite side. Base C on one side is always opposite and linked to base G on the other side. A single rung, therefore, can be:

- S-A-T-S
- S-T-A-S
- S-C-G-S
- S-G-C-S

KEY FACTS **SEX CHROMOSOMES AND CRIME**

There are two chromosomes that determine sex. The X chromosome comes from the mother, and is similar in size to the other chromosomes; the Y chromosome, from the father, is smaller. A pair of two X chromosomes results in a female, while an XY combination results in a male. Some males, however, are found to have a combination of three chromosomes, either XXY or XYY. Because the Y is connected with masculinity, it has been suggested that an XYY male would be a "supermale," more aggressive, and possibly criminal. However, recent studies have found no evidence that XYY males are more likely to commit violent crimes than normal XY men.

There are over 3 billion of these rungs in human DNA, and they are called **nucleotides** (*nu-clee-o-tides*). A number of nucleotides make up a gene. Genes provide specific codes or instructions. Ultimately, through a number of complicated processes, genes are translated into proteins—and almost everything in the body is made of proteins or made by them. In particular, proteins called **enzymes** trigger chemical reactions in the body. Genes also determine hereditary characteristics—as Thomas Hunt Morgan had suggested many decades before, even though he did not understand their structure or how they worked.

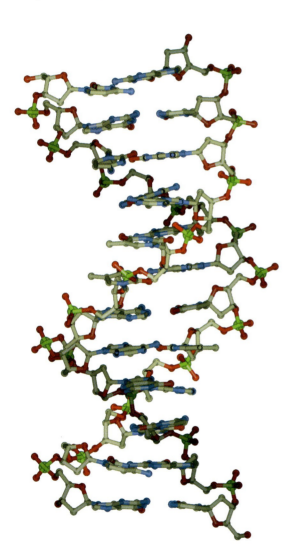

In humans and animals, many genes are identical—for example those that provide the code that ultimately leads to the development of two legs, two arms, two eyes, and so on, and even the order in which limbs and organs are created. In fact, approximately 99.5 percent of all DNA—those parts concerned with gene inheritance—is similar for everybody. It's the remaining 0.5 percent of DNA, however, that is of most interest to forensic scientists.

The detection of specific genes already allows forensic laboratories to provide a detailed physical description of, for example, an individual's sex, hair, eyes, and skin color. Other genes can indicate specific racial characteristics.

An illustration of a very short section of the DNA ladder. The yellow-colored five-sided groups are ribose. The gray and red groups are phosphate, and the purine "rungs" are colored red and green.

TOOLS **X-RAY CRYSTALLOGRAPHY**

When x-rays are directed at crystal, their atoms or molecular groups produce characteristic patterns on a piece of photographic film. This is because the individual components in crystal are held in a regular, rigid structure, at a fixed distance from one another. The molecules of DNA are also fixed in position and have a crystal-like structure. They can, therefore, be photographed in a similar way.

The Human Genome Project

As a result of The Human Genome Project, which completed its first stage in 2003, investigators have another more useful tool at their disposal. The project's purpose was to identify every nucleotide and all of the 20,000 to 30,000 genes running the entire length of a piece of human DNA. Project researchers discovered long stretches of nucleotides between the identified genes that appeared to play no part in heredity. These portions have been named "junk DNA." Despite the name, these portions of DNA probably play the most important role in allowing investigators to identify individuals using DNA analysis.

By 2006, the science of DNA analysis had advanced so far that British police were able to issue a description of a man they had been seeking for more than sixteen years. Since 1990, he had assaulted at least eighteen elderly women. Although investigators had samples of his DNA, no match could be found on the national database. Using DNA testing, the police established the criminal's genetic make-up to be 82 percent sub-Saharan African, 6 percent European, and 12 percent Native American, and that this DNA matched the characteristics of a man from the Windward Islands. In October 2006, investigating officers set off for the Caribbean in search of the criminal. At the time of writing, investigating officers were optimistic of finding either the offender or his family.

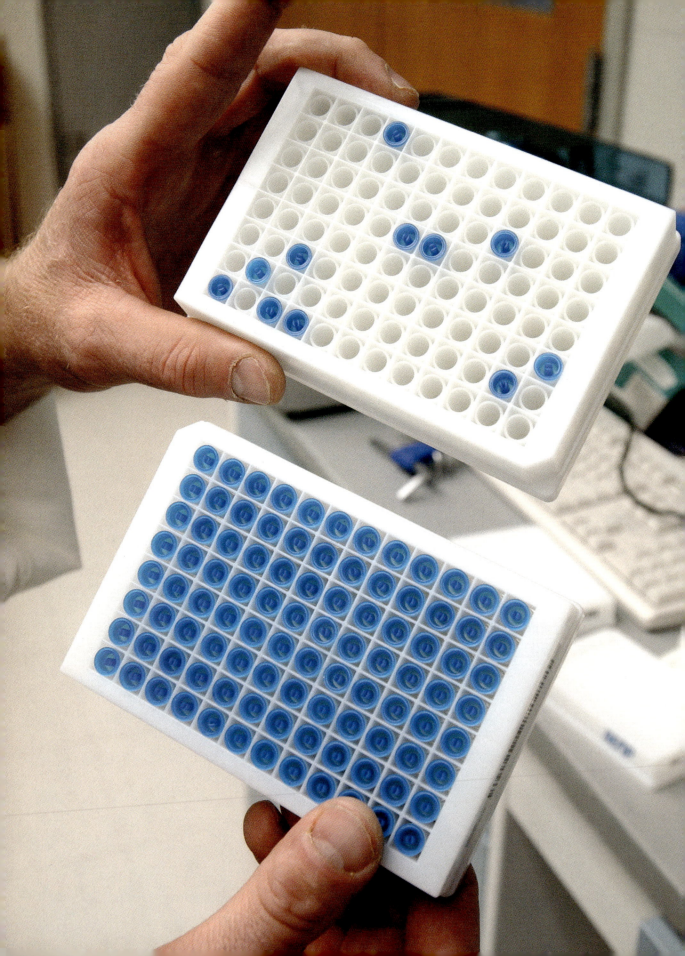

chapter 3

DNA Fingerprinting

A vital discovery made it possible to break the DNA molecule into short fragments, and so identify a single individual.

B y 1953, scientists understood DNA's chemical composition and structure. However, it still seemed an impossible task to identify a sample of one person's DNA because the 3 billion nucleotides (*see* Chapter 2, page 30) can combine in so many ways.

In 1970, American microbiologist Hamilton O. Smith discovered that bacteria produced enzymes to attack foreign DNA from viruses and protect themselves. These are called restriction enzymes. They each attack the strand of DNA at specific points, breaking off a short fragment of just a few nucleotides. Scientists have now identified more than 400 restriction enzymes, and each one cuts the DNA strand at a different place. (Hamilton Smith shared the 1978 Nobel Prize in Physiology with two other scientists for this work.)

The sides of the DNA ladder are made up of alternating S and P molecules (*see* Chapter 2, page 29). Each restriction

◁ **Modern DNA analysis kits are available from a number of commercial organizations. These plates can hold 96 samples for simultaneous analysis.**

enzyme cuts the ladder only at a specific place—known as a **locus** (plural: loci). For example, one restriction enzyme named Hae III, from the bacterium *Haemophilus aegyptius*, cuts the strand only at loci where it finds the sequence:

$$\text{-G} \quad \text{G} \quad \text{C} \quad \text{C-}$$
$$| \quad | \quad | \quad |$$
$$\text{-C} \quad \text{C} \quad \text{G} \quad \text{G-}$$

Between the two loci where this sequence occurs, Hae III releases a fragment of the DNA. By examining these fragments, it is possible to identify an individual because it is extremely unlikely that two people's DNA would have exactly the same sequences—other than identical twins. Members of the same family usually share a number of sequences, but there will also be many more differences.

The analysis of fragments of DNA is known as DNA typing.

DNA Typing

Modern laboratories use computerized equipment for DNA typing, but it is useful to know how the technique developed.

Each fragment of DNA varies in length—or, to be more precise, it has a different molecular size. Scientists use electrophoresis (*see* Chapter 1, page 14) to separate them. They place the fragments in a gel-coated plate and apply a low-voltage direct current to the plate. The current causes the fragments to move from one side of the plate to the other. They move at different speeds, depending on their size, the biggest being the slowest. Because the molecules move in a straight line, it is possible to place a number of samples side by side down the plate, for comparison. Gradually, the different fragments separate across the width of the plate.

In 1975, the Scottish scientist Edward Southern developed the next step in DNA fragment analysis—the Southern blot. The gel-coated plate is soaked in a solution that separates the double-stranded fragments into single strands. At the same time, the plate is pressed against a plastic membrane. The single strands are transferred to the membrane. The bases (*see* Chapter 2, page 27) of the nucleotide—A, C, G, and T—are exposed along the length of each half

TECHNOLOGY   MODERN INSTRUMENTATION

A typical computer printout from computerized analysis of DNA. The main peaks indicate specific fragments.

In RFLP analysis, a single piece of automated equipment has largely taken the place of autorads. Specific fluorescent chemicals color the fragments and, as each molecule band emerges from the electrophoresis stage, a laser scans it. A computer then analyzes the scan and produces a printout profile. On the printout, each peak (high point) represents a molecule. The peaks are very sharp and precise—like the recording of earthquakes on a seismograph. This graph is called a DNA profile.

Instead of gel plates, modern computer equipment uses a set of extremely fine tubes called capillaries. Because the tubes are very narrow, the molecular fragments move through them at different rates and separate in the same way as they do on a gel plate.

; CCAGGAGGT GCTGTGA...
G GCTCCCAGCT GCTGTGA... GCCAC...
CC CACTTCTGGT GCCCACTGTG GCCAC... AGA...
GGG GCCTCCTGGG GAGCTGCTGA CCCTAGGCAG AGA...
AGA CACCCCAGTG TTTGCCAGTG TTTGCCCGTG TTCACCAGTG T...
AGTA TTTGCTCGCC AGTGTTCGCC ACTTGTCCCT CTGGCTGCAA GAGTGACTG
GCGG GAAGTTGCAG GTCCCTCCAG GACAGTTGGC CGATGACGTG GAGACAGACC
CCCAA TCCTGGCTCC CTGCAGGACG CGGGGCCCCC CGAGATCCTG GCGGTGCTCA
GACGGG CACCTCCGTG TTCACCAGTC CAATGGGCAC GGAGCGTGGC TTTATTTGCA
TGGATT CCTAACGACT TCAGCCTCTG CACCTCCTGG GTTTTCCCTG CTGCAAATTG
TTTGGCG TCGTCCCCAA TTTCCGGCCA AGGCCGCGTC GTCGTGCTGC TGTGTAATTT
GTGTGGA GTTCTAGATA CCAAGTGTCT GTCGGTTTTA GACATCGCAA ACGTCCTTCC
GTGTGGCC CGTCCATTCG CTTCTGTGCA GCAAAATCTT TAATTATTTG ATGGCATCAA
ATGTGTGTC CAGTTTTACC TTCTAGTTTA TACTTTCGAA CATTTGTTTG AGAAATCTTT
TCCCACCTG TGGCTGATAG TGACGTCTTC TAACTTCCCA TTTACTATGT TACATTCAGA
CCCATCATCT TCAGGAAGAC GCTTGTGTGC GAGACGGGTA TGAGGCCCCC ACACCCCGCC
TCAGGACCAC TGTCCATGGT TCCACCCCTG ACCCCGGACT CCGCTCCCCA GACCTCCTA

The complete human genome can be detailed in terms of the purine bases that make up a separated single strand of DNA.

of the original fragment. They are then labeled with one or more probes. A probe is a short length of a single-strand DNA or RNA fragment that has been labeled with a **radioactive** atom. The bases in the probe find their matching bases in the fragment and attach themselves. In other words, base A in the probe attaches to base T in the fragment. Base G in the probe attaches to base C in the fragment. This process of finding and attaching is known as hybridizing.

The scientist then washes the plastic membrane and places it in contact with a sheet of x-ray photographic film, which is then developed. The radioactive probe produces an image on the film—an **autoradiograph** (autorad, for short). An autorad consists of short, dark bands across the film—similar to a barcode. Each band represents a specific fragment, and bands that are level with each other are of the same molecular size. This method is known as restriction fragment length polymorphism (RFLP).

A simpler form of RFLP uses probes that locate only one locus, which makes it easier to read the results. The drawback is that finding a match between only a few bands is not positive proof of identity. With the RFLP technique, it is also possible to find a *number* of fragments of DNA from different people that do match. As pointed out above, it is extremely unlikely that two or more people will have a *high number* of identical sequences in their DNA. Nevertheless, the possibility does exist, which has raised some legal questions about the admissibility of some DNA as evidence (*see* Chapter 6).

DNA Fingerprinting

In 1984, in England, Alec Jeffreys developed the technique known as DNA fingerprinting, which is a variation on RFLP analysis. Jeffreys examined strands of DNA to see if they had identical base sequences along their length, for example:

C-G-G-A-T-C-G-G-A-T-C-G-G-A-T

The above sequence has three repeated base sequence patterns. He also found that the number of repeated base sequences could vary from one locus to another. For this reason, he called the technique **variable number tandem repeats** (VNTR). Jeffreys claims that the technique can identify a single individual among 1,000 trillion trillion trillion people—many times greater than the entire population of the world. It was not long before VNTR was put to the test in a real criminal case.

In June 1987, a burglar broke into a house in Bristol, England and attacked a disabled woman, then stole her jewelry. Investigators managed to obtain a sample of the attacker's DNA from the victim.

Some time later, police arrested Robert Melias for another burglary in the same district. They then invited the victim of the first break-in and assault to attend an identity lineup. She identified the arrested man as her attacker. Using the VNTR technique for the first time in a criminal case, the DNA sample taken at the time of the attack matched Melias' DNA. At trial in November 1987, he was found guilty and sentenced to eighteen years in prison. The case established a precedent for DNA evidence, making it admissible in English law.

In November 1987 also, the trial of Tommy Lee Andrews was heard in Florida. Between May and December 1986, Orlando police were faced with twenty-three cases of prowling, breaking and entering, and assault. The man would stalk his victim for several weeks, peeping through her windows and studying her daily routine, so that he could figure out the best time to enter her home.

The crimes continued into 1987, and in March the police arrested Andrews. From his fingerprints, and from his victims' partial descriptions, investigators identified Andrews as the attacker. His ABO blood type (*see* Chapter 1, page 14) also matched samples from the attacks. However, in the case of his first victim, who had positively identified him, Andrews had an apparently unshakable alibi. He said he had been at home with his sister and girlfriend on the night in question.

The prosecuting attorney had read an advertisement for DNA typing by the Lifecodes Corporation, so he requested an RFLP comparison of Andrews' blood and the samples from the attacks. They matched, and at a pre-trial hearing the judge agreed that the evidence was admissible. Unfortunately, the prosecutor was not familiar with the significance of the technique. As a result, he made

DNA samples can be stored in a semi-frozen state for later analysis.

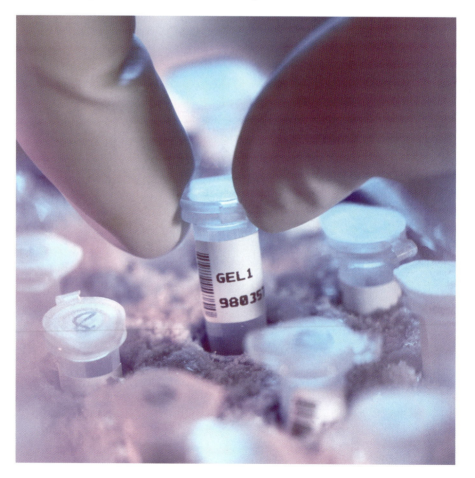

such sweeping claims in court about the probability of positive identification using RFLP evidence that the defense challenged his figures. The jury was undecided, and a mistrial declared.

When it came to retrial in February 1988, the prosecution had properly prepared its case. Expert witnesses carefully explained DNA typing to the court. Andrews was convicted and sentenced to twenty-eight years for his first attack, together with twenty-two years for another attack, twenty-two for robbery, and fifteen for burglary. The appeal court upheld both the judge's ruling on DNA evidence and the conviction.

With these two cases established, the way was open for a rapid expansion in the use of DNA typing in evidence. Soon, forensic investigators all over the world had adopted the technique.

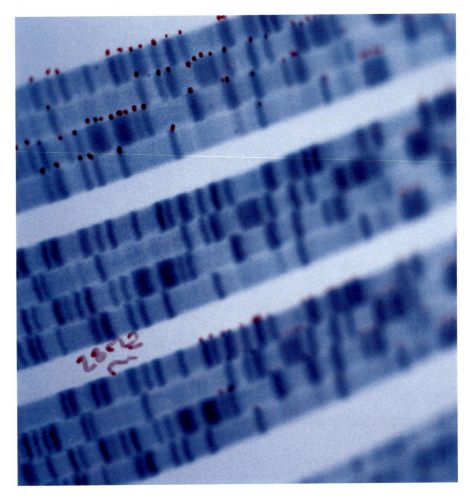

A section of a typical autorad, produced as part of the research into the human genome.

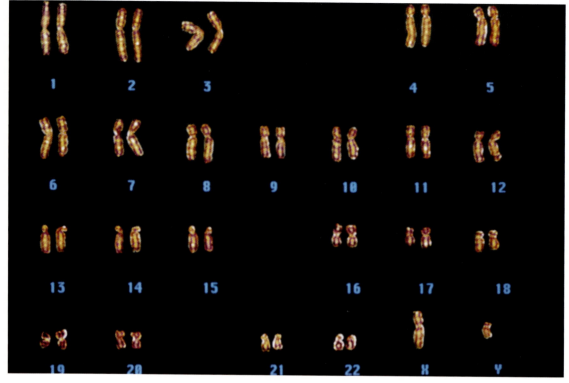

The twenty-three pairs of chromosomes that determine every aspect of human heredity. The Y chromosome involved in the determination of sex is noticeably smaller.

Innocent or Guilty?

Even before its legal acceptance, DNA fingerprinting proved its value, not only in establishing one person's guilt, but also in proving another's innocence.

On the evening of November 21, 1983, Lynda Mann, aged fifteen, failed to return home in the village of Narborough, in the English Midlands. Next morning, her body was discovered beside a footpath near a hospital. She had been strangled with her own scarf.

Examination revealed that the killer was a secretor (*see* Chapter 1, page 15) of blood type A/PGM1+. In other words, the attacker had blood group A, associated with the enzyme phosphoglucomutase (*foss-fo-gluco-mu-tase*) type 1. (At this time, Jeffreys' work on DNA fingerprinting was still in development.) About 10 percent of the male British population was of this type. The police, however, had good reasons to narrow their search to males between the ages of thirteen and thirty-four. However, despite extensive inquiries by a 150-strong investigating force, and a search through the records of all known local sex offenders, they could not find a firm suspect. In August 1984, they suspended the investigation.

On August 2, 1986, the body of Dawn Ashworth, also fifteen years old, was found in similar circumstances, close by the same hospital. Police were soon convinced that the same man had committed both murders.

At the time of Lynda's death, police had questioned fourteen-year-old Richard Buckland, who was a notorious local criminal. He was big for his age, not very intelligent, and was known to frighten females by suddenly jumping out of hiding at them. By 1986, Buckland, now seventeen, was working as a janitor in the psychiatric hospital. On August 8, police arrested and interrogated him. After two days of rambling and inconsistent admissions, Buckland signed a confession to the murder of Ashworth, but denied that he was responsible for Mann's death. His trial was set for November 21 of that year.

The police asked Jeffreys to carry out analysis of a blood sample from Buckland, together with stored samples from the two murdered girls. After several weeks, Jeffreys reported that one man had indeed committed both murders—but it was definitely not Buckland. There was no evidence for a trial.

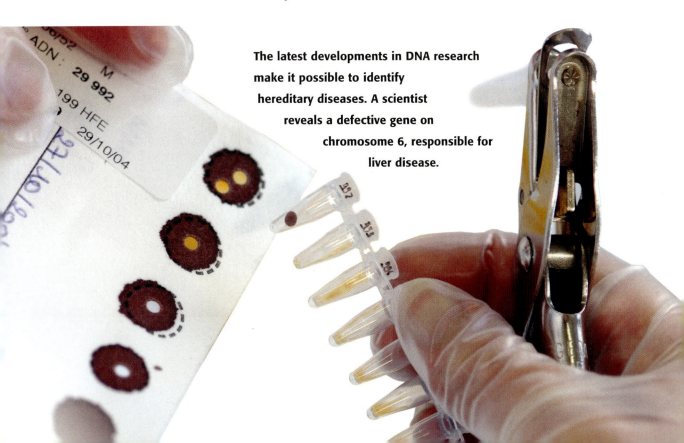

The latest developments in DNA research make it possible to identify hereditary diseases. A scientist reveals a defective gene on chromosome 6, responsible for liver disease.

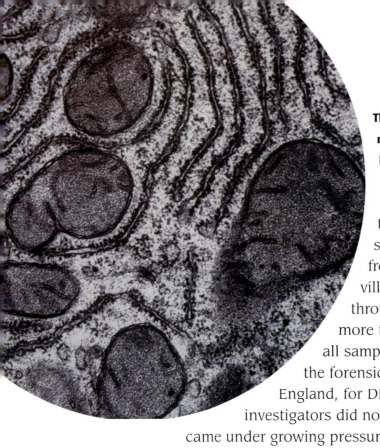

This photograph, taken by an electron microscope, reveals the small round bodies of the mitochondria.

Faced with this setback, the police decided to collect samples of blood and saliva from all the young males of the villages in the area. From January through September 1987, they took more than 5,000 samples. They sent all samples from A/PGM1+ secretors to the forensic laboratory at Aldermaston, England, for DNA typing. When forensic investigators did not find a single match, the police came under growing pressure to end the investigation.

Then, during a conversation at a bar, a local bakery worker mentioned that a colleague, Colin Pitchfork, age twenty-seven, had paid him to give a blood sample in his place. Pitchfork had a previous conviction and had also been an outpatient at the psychiatric hospital. Police had questioned him at the time of Mann's death, although he had come to live in the area after that date. They now arrested him, and his blood DNA was found to be a positive match.

On January 22, 1988, Pitchfork pleaded guilty in a trial that lasted only a single day. He was sentenced to two terms of life imprisonment for murder, and ten years for each assault.

PCR—Multiplying the DNA

A principal drawback of RFLP is that it requires a fairly large DNA sample for analysis. Sometimes the traces obtained from a crime scene—a single hair, for example—are too small. Also, much of the DNA, even in a reasonably sized sample, may already have begun to break down into long fragments. Exposure to sunlight, contamination by microorganisms such as bacteria, temperature changes, and the effects of various chemical substances can all cause DNA to **degrade**.

In 1983, American Kary Mullis provided the answer to both these problems. At that time, Mullis was working for the Cetus Corporation, which has been among the frontrunners in genome research.

Mullis developed a technique called polymerase chain reaction (PCR) (see Chapter 4, pages 52–53). This technique uses an enzyme—polymerase—that copies single DNA strands or, equally importantly, fragments of degraded DNA. The two strands are then copied again, producing four, and so on, in a chain reaction that can produce a million or more copies within only a few hours. The copies can then be analyzed. Forensic scientists claim that even a single strand can be enough to start the PCR process. For this reason, people have often described it as molecular photocopying. Mullis was awarded the Nobel Prize in 1993 for this discovery.

STR

RFLP is detailed and precise, but it takes time—sometimes weeks. Shortly after the introduction of PCR, analysts turned to a much quicker detection method that uses units only three, four, or five nucleotides long. The method is known as **short tandem repeats** (STRs).

The great advantage of modern systems based on the PCR technique is that they can now identify as many as sixteen loci, and the process is largely automated. Simple PCR kits are now available to many law enforcement agencies in the United States, and even relatively inexperienced technicians can use them. However, these are only preliminary tests: the enzyme used in these kits targets only a single kind of locus, and so can discriminate between only just a few individuals.

Identifying the Individual

DNA analysis requires a sample from the crime scene—blood, hair, any of the several body fluids, or even a fingerprint—for comparison with the DNA of a suspect. Since nearly every cell of the body contains DNA, it is not necessary to take blood from the suspect. Often, it is enough to pluck a few hairs from the head, or take a swab of the cells inside the mouth—the **epithelial** cells. Even when two samples match, forensic evidence of this kind must be regarded with caution. It has taken time, particularly in the United States, for the courts to accept it.

In pinpointing an individual, the more loci that can be identified, the better. If only a few loci are detected, then the laws of probability need to come into play to evaluate the evidence. For example, investigators obtain four fragments of DNA from a crime scene. They match all four fragments to a suspect. However, these fragments of DNA occur in the general population as follows:

- Fragment one: 42 in 100
- Fragment two: 32 in 100
- Fragment three: 2 in 100
- Fragment four: 1 in 100

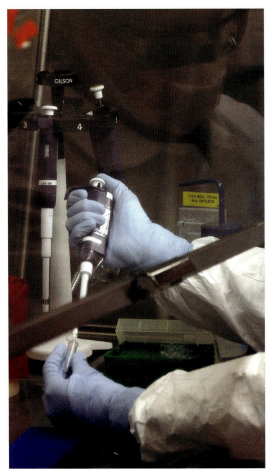

Therefore, the probability of obtaining all four fragments from a single sample is:

42 x 32 x 2 x 1 = 2,688 in 100 million, or approximately 1 in 37,000

This is much less than the "one in 30 million" figures claimed for RFLP and STR evidence in early court cases. The obvious conclusion is that with DNA evidence, it is important to detect more loci for greater accuracy.

There are added difficulties when it comes to calculating how frequently specific DNA loci occur in population groups. For example, a specific gene

A U.S. Defense Department laboratory technician about to analyze mitochondrial DNA taken from a bone fragment. The bone was believed to be from an American man missing in action, and analysis could establish his identity.

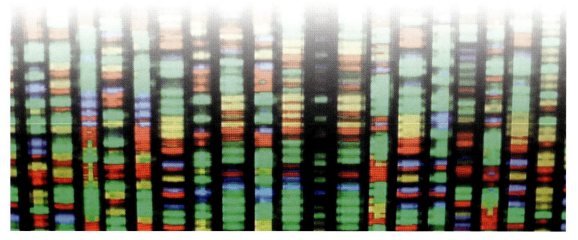

A digital representation of a portion of the human genome. The four types of molecule that make up each nucleotide have been colored differently to distinguish them.

determines whether someone is born with blood type B (*see* Chapter 1, page 13). Looking at a map of Europe, the percentages of people who have this gene are as follows:

- Britain, France, Spain, Italy, Germany, and Scandinavia: 5–10 percent
- Western Russia: 15–20 percent
- Northern Siberia: 25–30 percent

Clearly, there is a need for detailed population statistics—which are being collated, but only gradually. Calculations also need to be accurate with regard to the characteristics of local populations, and not just based on national averages. Otherwise, statistical estimates may be challenged in court (*see* Chapter 6, page 80).

Mitochondrial DNA

The **ovum** cell contains a considerable number of bodies much smaller than the nucleus (*see* Chapter 2, page 25). These are the **mitochondria** (*mit-o-kon-dria*), which are responsible for generating energy in cells. The male sperm cell also contains mitochondria but only in its tail, which breaks away at the moment of conception. As the embryo develops, however, the female mitochondria are copied into each dividing cell.

Early on in gene research, scientists discovered that the mitochondria contain a very different form of DNA—known as mtDNA—which is shorter in length and generally circular in structure. Unlike regular DNA, which is a combination of genes from both father and mother, mtDNA remains unchanged from generation to generation. With the development of RFLP and VNTR DNA typing techniques, there once seemed little point researching the forensic possibilities of mtDNA— as it comes only from the mother. Recently, however, mtDNA analysis has proved invaluable.

Death of a Tsar

Following the Russian Revolution in 1917, the ruler of Russia, Tsar Nicholas II, his wife, the Tsarina Alexandra, and their five children—the family Romanov—were imprisoned in a house in Ekaterinburg (later named Sverdlovsk), Siberia. On the night of July 16, 1918, the family, their doctor, and servants—eleven people in all—were executed by a local firing squad. In the 1960s, the Soviet government appointed Nikolas Sokolov to investigate the exact circumstances. He reported that the bodies had been thrown down an abandoned mineshaft, soaked in sulfuric acid, and finally destroyed by fire. In 1989, however, a filmmaker named Gely Ryabov announced that he had discovered bones and scraps of clothing in a bog about 5 miles (8 kilometers) from the mine. In 1991, the Soviet president, Boris Yeltsin, authorized the excavation of the site. Investigators unearthed about 1,000 pieces of bones and skulls, together with fourteen bullets, pieces of rope, and a jar that had once contained sulfuric acid.

Forensic anthropologists painstakingly assembled the remains into nine skeletons—four male and five female. Russian experts identified the skulls, and decided that the missing two were those of the Tsar's son, Alexei, and his daughter, Marie. However, a team of American experts, headed by leading forensic anthropologist Dr. William R. Maples, suggested that one missing skull might be that of another daughter, Anastasia.

Recent advances in PCR analysis have made it possible to extract DNA material from bones. In 1993, Pavel Ivanov, head of the DNA unit of the Russian Academy of Sciences, took sample bones to the British Forensic Science Service. There, Dr. Peter Gill extracted mtDNA and multiplied it using PCR. A leading member of the British Royal Family, the Duke of Edinburgh, provided a sample of his own blood. His mtDNA matched the mtDNA of one of the samples—identifying the remains as those of his great aunt, the Tsarina. The Tsar's brother's tomb was then opened and a positive DNA match obtained from the bones. Dr. Mary-Claire King at University College Berkeley confirmed the results.

CASE STUDY **A ROYAL DYNASTY**

Although it was long believed that eleven people from the Russian royal family were killed in Ekaterinburg, only nine skeletons were recovered. For many years, there were rumors that Alexei and Anastasia had somehow escaped execution. A woman calling herself Anna Anderson, who died in the United States in 1984, had claimed all her life that she was the missing Anastasia. She was cremated, so it was impossible to obtain DNA from her bones. However, it turned out that an American hospital had retained samples of her tissue, following a surgical operation. In 1994, DNA typing showed that she was not a Romanov. She was a Polish peasant named Franzisca Shcanzkowska. Members of the Schanzkowska family provided DNA samples to confirm this.

The Russian royal family, photographed some years before their assassination. The Tsar, in army uniform, stands to the left, and Anastasia is the girl on the right.

The Crime Scene

At the scene of a crime, it is essential that any DNA trace evidence should be handled with great care, and submitted for detailed analysis.

S amples of DNA can be left at a crime scene in many ways. If, for example, there has been a struggle, the perpetrator may have bled, leaving traces on surfaces, objects, or even the victim. If he tied or strangled his victim, he may have left skin cells on a rope or ligature (anything from a cord or a strap to a necktie).

If his victim bit him in the struggle, there may be traces in the victim's mouth. Discarded cigarette butts, saliva, or spots where he urinated can also contain DNA. In cases involving physical assault, body fluids and body hairs are particularly important. Sometimes—particularly in cases of abduction—the criminal will later use a public telephone, either to demand a ransom or to taunt the police. If investigators can trace the telephone, they can take swabs of saliva from the mouthpiece, as well as fingerprints.

◁ **Forensic examiners collecting DNA trace evidence at a crime scene. They are properly dressed in full-body protective suits and gloves, and wear masks to avoid contaminating the evidence by breathing or coughing on the material.**

PROCEDURE NIJ CHECKLIST

The United States National Institute of Justice (NIJ) publishes a checklist of typical trace evidence that law enforcement officers should collect at a crime scene and other locations connected with it:

- fingernails or fingernail parings
- tissues, paper towels, napkins, cotton swabs, ear swabs (bag everything in a bathroom wastebasket)
- toothpicks, cigarette butts, straws, anything else that might have been in contact with the mouth, such as cellular phones
- blankets, pillows, sheets, mattresses, and dirty laundry
- headgear of any type (it can be examined for sweat or loose hairs)
- eyeglasses, contact lenses
- used stamps, envelopes
- tapes, ropes, cords, or anything else used as ligatures
- used condoms
- bullets that have passed through bodies

In its publication *What Every Law Enforcement Officer Should Know About DNA Evidence*, the NIJ points out:

Remember that just because you cannot see a stain does not mean there are not enough cells for DNA typing. Further, DNA does more than just identify the source of the sample; it can place a known individual at a crime scene, in a home, or in a room where the suspect claimed not to have been. It can refute a claim of self-defense and put a weapon in the suspect's hand. It can change a story from an alibi to one of consent.

Wearing the appropriate full-body protective suits, British police crime scene investigators search for evidence at the burial site of a murder victim near a river in northern England.

Collecting Evidence

Because it is automated and produces results quickly, the PCR-STR process is now the usual method of DNA typing employed in forensic laboratories in the United States. However, because the process means that all DNA examined is **amplified**, whatever its source, samples can be corrupted. Crime scene investigators must take great care when collecting trace evidence. Laboratories must follow very strict procedures to keep each piece of evidence separate and ensure that the chain of custody is logged from individual to individual. It is also vital that investigators are not contaminated by the samples. **Biohazards** such as **hepatitis** and **HIV** are particularly dangerous, so they must wear gloves at all times, frequently changing and disposing of them safely.

The NIJ (National Institute of Justice) recommends the use of disposable tools where possible. If that is not possible, the instruments should be cleaned thoroughly before and after taking each sample. Other commonsense recommendations, which also apply to laboratory workers, include:

- Avoid touching the area where you believe DNA exists
- Avoid talking, sneezing, and coughing over evidence
- Avoid touching your face, nose, and mouth when collecting and packaging evidence

Each item of evidence should be dried in the air before being packaged, so that it does not degrade unnecessarily on the way to the laboratory. The evidence should be put into new paper bags or envelopes, not into plastic bags or containers, and the bags must not be closed with staples.

PCR–STR Analysis

The original polymerase chain reaction (PCR) technique (*see* Chapter 3, pages 42–43) developed by Kary Mullis followed three stages, which could be performed even in a laboratory test tube. This technique, though, was soon replaced by a piece of equipment called a **thermal cycler**. First, the sample is put in a suitable chemical solution and heated to 203˚F (95˚C). This splits the double

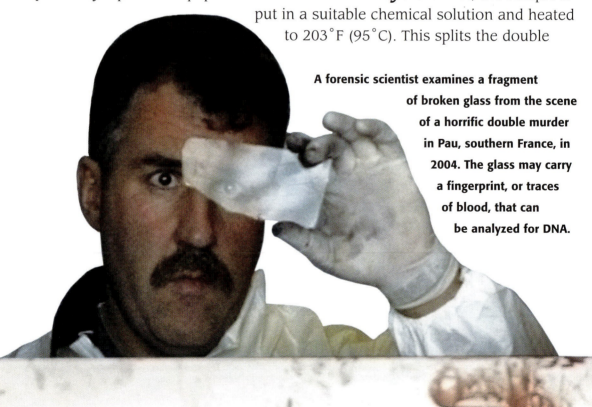

A forensic scientist examines a fragment of broken glass from the scene of a horrific double murder in Pau, southern France, in 2004. The glass may carry a fingerprint, or traces of blood, that can be analyzed for DNA.

Analysis for liver disease no longer requires a biopsy – a tissue sample taken from within the organ. Genetic analysis of the DNA allows the identification of the responsible gene, which is multiplied by PCR.

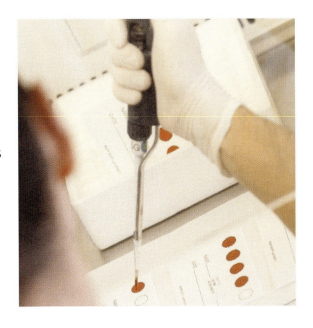

strands into single strands, regardless of their length. The heat is then reduced to around 100° F (38° C), and a supply of A, C, G, and T (adenine, cytosine, guanine, and thymine—*see* Chapter 2, page 27) bases are added, together with DNA primers. Primers are similar to probes and prevent the single strands from recombining. As the liquid cools, polymerase is added to make double strand copies of the single strands. So, from each original double strand, there are now two identical strands. The cycle is then repeated. After twenty cycles, the strands have been amplified to produce more than a million copies.

At first, this was a fairly inefficient process, because the first stage—the heating stage—destroyed the polymerase. Scientists then started to use a new polymerase called Taq, which comes from a microorganism, *Thermus aquaticus*, and survives the near boiling point of natural hot springs. Because Taq is not affected in the heating stage, it became possible to automate the entire process.

The first PCR kits were fairly simple. Dots of the amplified DNA material were fixed to strips of material. Specific markers then caused them to hybridize. A chemical dye turned the dots red, indicating a positive result. Later, a "reverse dot" technique was developed. The strips were dotted with the markers, and the amplified product hybridized with them. Later, another dye was used, which turned the dot blue. Since 1985, scientists have developed many far more complex techniques, and a number of independent commercial laboratories produce a range of kits. It is now possible to analyze as many as ninety-six samples simultaneously.

For a brief period during the 1990s, some forensic laboratories employed another system that was similar to variable number tandem repeats (VNTR)

FORENSIC ANALYSIS **UNUSUAL TRACES**

In a recent case, a researcher took a flea found in a suspect's clothing, analyzed the DNA in the blood in the insect's stomach, and matched it to that of the victim. This, of course, was not positive evidence, but it at least placed suspect and victim in close proximity to each other at some time.

Pollen from crime scenes has been matched to pollen detected on stolen vehicles. Researchers now hope that they will soon be able to match bacteria and virus samples to determine whether two individuals have been in the same environment.

analysis (*see* Chapter 3, page 37). This system could detect a smaller fragment that could then be amplified using PCR. The technique also used gel electrophoresis, but used silver to stain the bands, instead of autorads (*see* Chapter 3, page 35).

PCR, followed by short tandem repeats (STR) identification (*see* Chapter 3, page 43), is the accepted technique in the United States, but it is not as precise as restriction fragment length polymorphism (RFLP), which remains the standard in Britain and other countries. Nevertheless, the latest developments in this method raise the probability of a positive match to at least one in a million.

Victims of Disaster

DNA profiles—as the succession of peaks provided by the computer output are called—are not only vitally important in identifying a criminal. They can also help to identify unknown corpses or scattered remains from a disaster. Investigators used the STR technique to identify the victims of the Valujet crash in the Everglades, in May 1996, and those who died in the Branch Davidian fire outside Waco on April 19, 1993.

When the twin towers of the World Trade Center collapsed on September 11, 2001, the bodies of most of the victims disintegrated, making identification extremely difficult. Once again, in many cases, DNA analysis would be the only way to identify the dead and provide closure for their relatives.

On October 2, 2001, the National Institute of Justice called a meeting of genetic experts in New York. Representatives from the five laboratories that would be performing the DNA profiling attended, and a Kinship and Data Analysis Panel (KADAP) was set up. One member, Dr. Charles Brenner, undertook to develop a satisfactory computer program to analyze the results.

Investigators then began the work of separating the remains of an estimated 2,792 victims from the vast mounds of debris delivered to the Fresh Kills landfill facility. The first two successful identifications were of identical twins, but after just a further thirty positive matches, it was clear the program was not up to the

The task of identification of all the victims of the 2001 destruction of the World Trade Center continues, and it is hoped that more advanced techniques of analysis will prove successful. Here, the assistant director of Forensic Biology for the Chief Medical Examiner of NYC examines a body fragment recovered from the ruins.

huge task of successfully identifying remains from the masses of rubble and debris. What was needed was more detailed data on family relationships and the recovery of more remains.

Then, even as KADAP was discussing the problem, an American Airlines plane crashed in Queens on November 12, 2001. Within weeks, most of the victims of the Queens crash were identified. A detailed examination of the data relating to the victims' family relations made it possible to modify and improve Brenner's original computer software. As a result, it became possible to identify many more fragments of DNA from the Trade Center disaster.

Excavation of the World Trade Center was officially concluded on May 30, 2002. In June 2003, the New York chief medical examiner announced the identification of the 1,500th victim. About 800 were named using DNA analysis, often by samples provided by relatives, such as hair from a brush. He said that his target was to reach 2,000—but this could depend upon the further development of DNA techniques.

By September 2006, 1,641 victims had been named but, out of 20,730 fragments sifted from the debris, 9,797 had still not been identified. This included 760 fragments only recently discovered atop the Deutsche Bank building at the site. In the same month, the medical examiner's office signed a new contract with Cybergenetics, a Pittsburgh company, to perform further tests. The company, using recently developed technology, claimed to be able to carry out analysis 1,000 times faster than previous methods.

A Cold Case Re-opened

Shortly after midday on December 26, 1996, John Ramsey discovered the body of his young daughter, JonBenet, in the basement of their home in Boulder, Colorado. She had been assaulted and strangled. Her mother, Patsy, had earlier telephoned the police to say that her daughter had been kidnapped, and that a ransom note had been left at the foot of the stairs.

Several aspects of the murder convinced the Boulder police that JonBenet's parents were the prime suspects. In particular, they stated that there were no signs of an intruder in the home. Much later, however, they admitted that there were several boot prints that could not be explained. Even though no positive evidence could be produced against the Ramseys, the media put forward many

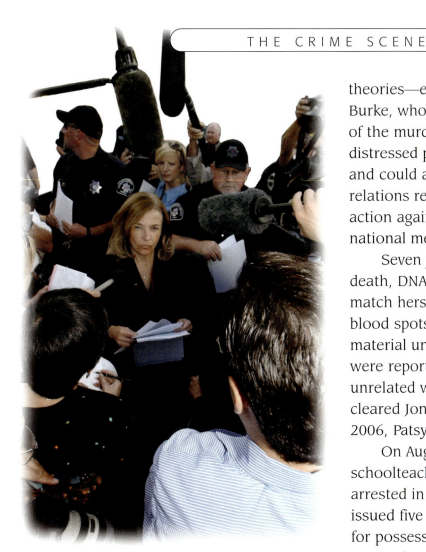

In August 2006, a spokesperson for the Colorado state court announced that charges against John Mark Karr in connection with the murder of JonBenet Ramsey had been dropped, after his DNA had been found to be inconsistent with evidence.

theories—even JonBenet's brother Burke, who was only nine at the time of the murder, has been accused. The distressed parents—who were rich, and could afford legal and public relations representation—took legal action against a number of leading national media companies.

Seven years after JonBenet's death, DNA profiles that did not match hers were at last obtained from blood spots in her clothing, and from material under her fingernails. They were reported to be from an unrelated white male, a result that cleared JonBenet's parents. In June 2006, Patsy Ramsey died.

On August 16, 2006, a former schoolteacher, John Mark Karr, was arrested in Thailand, on a warrant issued five years earlier in Colorado, for possession of child pornography. He confessed that he was responsible for JonBenet's death—claiming it was an accident—but ten days later the Colorado district attorney announced that Karr's DNA did not match the sample found on JonBenet's clothes. He was declared innocent of the murder. Over the years, private detectives have continued to investigate the case. They discovered that thirty-eight registered sex offenders lived within a 2-mile (3-kilometer) radius of the Ramsey home. Many of these men were also burglars. The investigators named many possible suspects, and provided details linking some of them to the Ramseys. So far, none of those named has provided a DNA match, and the investigation continues.

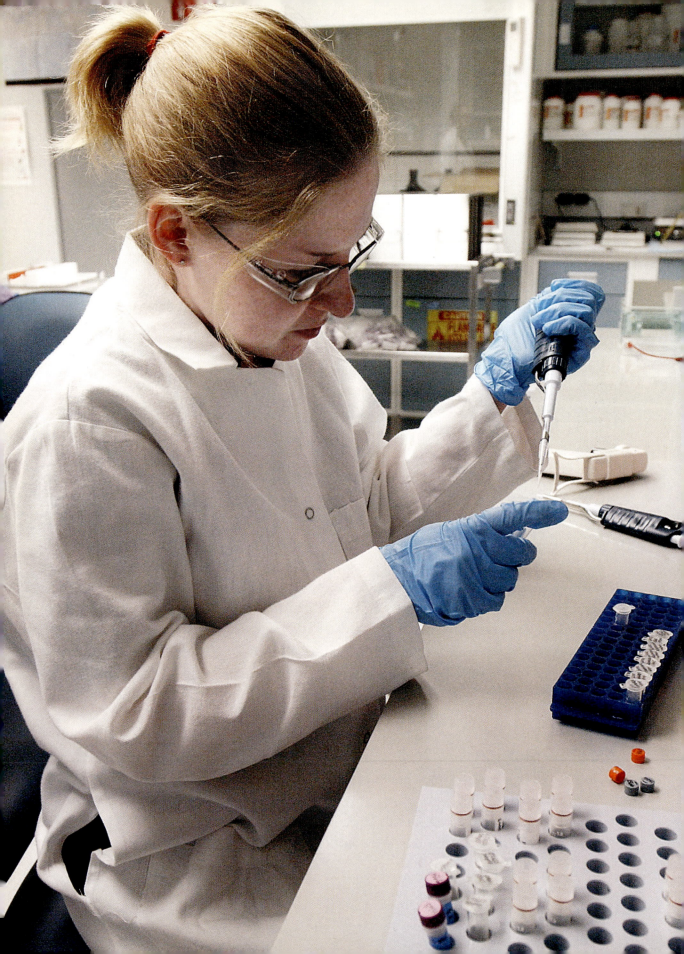

DNA Casebook

The value of DNA analysis has been proved in many cases. Scientific and technological advances continue to add to this field.

Over the past twenty-five years, the techniques of DNA analysis have made great advances. Although fingerprint identification remains the most successful of all forensic methods, DNA profiling has proved of great value in criminal investigations. It is important to remember that **geneticists** did much of the early work in developing forensic DNA techniques, and it is geneticists who continue research into other fields. A review of some key cases, criminal and otherwise, shows how far the forensic work has come along.

Murder Without a Corpse

It is a common belief that a person cannot be charged with murder unless there is a body—but this is not true. When Helen McCourt, age twenty-two, from Lancashire, England, went missing on February 9, 1988, DNA samples pointed to the killer.

◁ **A scientist carefully preparing DNA samples for computerized analysis.**

Bar owner Ian Simms is led into a waiting police van, after his conviction to life imprisonment for the murder of Helen McCourt.

Helen was last seen walking 300 yards (270 meters) from a bus stop to her home in the village of Billinge. Investigators searched all the premises along her route and questioned all the inhabitants. Inquiries centered on the local bar, where Helen was a regular customer, and in particular on the landlord, Ian Simms.

In Simms's car the police found a bloodstained earring that had belonged to Helen, and some strands of hair. Inside the bar, there was a trail of blood, and the clip from the earring, but there were no clues to where Helen's body might be found—if, in fact, she was dead.

Three weeks later, Helen's clothes and her purse were found on the bank of a river near the city of Manchester, some 25 miles (40 kilometers) to the east. An intensive police search of the area uncovered a man's clothing, heavily stained with blood, dumped 3 miles (5 kilometers) away. It belonged to Simms, who claimed that the killer—if there was a killer—must have stolen the clothing and worn it. However, hairs from his dogs, and carpet fibers from his room, were stuck to Helen's coat. There were also hairs caught in a length of electric cord found at the crime scene, which matched those in the car.

FORENSIC ANALYSIS   A PREHISTORIC ANCESTOR

DNA profiling has many more uses than criminal and paternity cases. Archaeologists, for example, now use very sensitive modern techniques to investigate kinship relations in ancient remains. In spring 1997, a team of scientists wanted to discover whether the DNA from a prehistoric skull, found in a cave in Somerset, England, belonged to an ancestor of anyone still living in the area. They asked local schoolchildren to provide blood samples. To set a good example for the children one of the schoolteachers also gave a sample.

No matches were found among the children, but the teacher was astounded to discover that he was, without doubt, a descendant of the man in the cave.

It was DNA from a prehistoric skull, like this, that revealed how the modern-day British schoolteacher was descended from his ancient ancestor.

Had Simms murdered Helen? Her body was never found, and there was no way her blood could be matched with that on Simms's clothes. At the time, DNA typing was still very new, so it was not yet possible, for example, to analyze hair from her brush, or saliva from a glass.

However, the forensic experts obtained blood samples from Helen's mother and father. They declared that the DNA of the blood on the clothing was 126,000 times more likely to have come from their daughter than from another person. Although Simms continued to insist that he had been framed, he was found guilty of murder on March 14, 1989, and given a life sentence.

Betrayed by a Hair

One of the most notorious serial killers of recent times was the Austrian Jack Unterweger. In this case, the DNA analysis of a single hair set off a trail leading through five countries in Europe, and across the world to Canada and the United States.

Unterweger was born in Styria, southeast Austria, in 1951, the son of an Austrian prostitute and an American soldier serving with the occupation troops. From an early age, he revealed an unpredictable temper—almost certainly born of a hatred of his mother's profession. At just sixteen, he was charged with an assault on a woman. Between 1967 and 1975, he gained sixteen convictions—mostly for attacks on women—and spent almost all of that time in prison. In 1976, he was at last convicted of murder, having beaten a prostitute with an iron bar, and then strangled her with her own clothing. At his trial, he told the judge: "I envisioned my mother in front of me, and I killed her."

Sentenced to life imprisonment, Unterweger began writing poems, plays, short stories, and an autobiography. He became famous in Austria, and when paroled in 1990 he took up journalism, announcing: "That life is over. Let's get on with the new." He quickly became a TV personality and a welcome guest at social events. He wrote press articles about prostitution in Austria, and even interviewed the police about a succession of murders of prostitutes that occurred over a twelve-month period—murders, it was later established, that he had committed.

In June 1991, an Austrian magazine commissioned Unterweger to write about crime in Los Angeles. While there, he rode several times with the police in patrol

Serial killer Jack Unterweger, arrested in Miami in 1993. Originally jailed in Austria for murder in 1976, he became a media star on his release in 1990. But he continued his fatal career, and was soon sought by police in four countries.

cars. In this same period, three local prostitutes were murdered, beaten, and strangled with their own clothing. In each case, their bodies were found out in the open, near downtown hotels where Unterweger had stayed.

When he returned to Austria, the police were still investigating the murders of six women whose bodies had been found in woods around Vienna. Interpol alerted investigators that the crimes were very similar to those committed in Los Angeles. On his release from prison in 1990, Unterweger had bought a BMW car, but he then sold it and bought a VW Passat. The police were able to trace the buyer of the BMW, who allowed them to search it. They found a woman's hair. Dr. Manfred Hochmeister, at the Insitut für Rechtsmedizin in Berne, Switzerland, was asked to carry out a polymerase chain reaction (PCR) analysis (*see* Chapter 3, pages 42–43). He identified the hair as belonging to one of the murdered prostitutes. Police obtained a warrant to search Unterweger's apartment, where they found a menu from a restaurant in Malibu and photographs of the journalist posing with women members of the Los Angeles Police Department (LAPD). By then, however, Unterweger had left, traveling with his girlfriend through Switzerland, France, and Canada, before reaching the United States again. A trail of credit card receipts led to Miami, Florida, where he was eventually captured.

After long legal arguments, the U.S. administration agreed to allow Unterweger to be tried in Austria—provided that the American killings were taken into account—and he was extradited to the Austrian city of Graz. At his trial in 1994, the court heard that Unterweger had, in little more than two years since his release from prison, murdered eleven women—six in Austria, three in Los Angeles, and two more in Czechoslovakia. He was found guilty of nine of the eleven murders but, a few hours later, he was discovered dead in his cell. He had strangled himself with the drawstring from his sweatpants.

A Deadly Guard

Even if a detailed DNA profile can be obtained from the scene of crime, it is of little use until it can be matched to DNA from a suspect. Also, other evidence must be presented at trial before a conviction is considered safe.

Early on the morning of October 7, 1990, the body of Louise Kaplan, a fashion photographer, age thirty-four, was found lying among trash cans in an alley between two hotels in central Manhattan, New York. She had been assaulted and strangled.

This was the third similar attack in that part of Manhattan in little more than three weeks. Louise's car was parked 50 yards (45 meters) away, and there were signs that a struggle had taken place inside. Impressions on the rear seat showed that someone had been sitting there. The murderer had probably

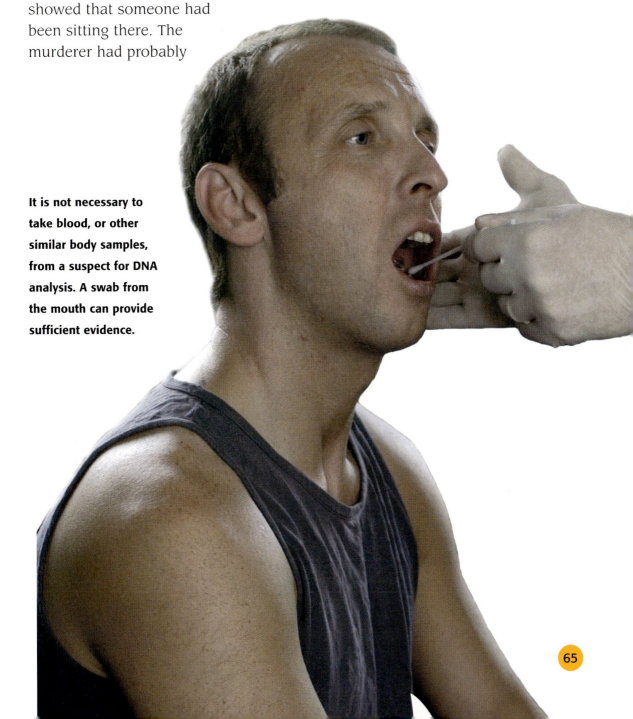

It is not necessary to take blood, or other similar body samples, from a suspect for DNA analysis. A swab from the mouth can provide sufficient evidence.

65

waited for Louise to return, and then attacked her. She had managed to escape from the car but got trapped in the alley, where she had tried to fight off her assailant before being overcome.

Evidence Trail

The police were sure that the same man had committed both previous crimes. DNA typing confirmed their hunch. Strangely, though, analysis of samples taken from Louise's body was unsuccessful. However, among the piles of trash collected from the scene for analysis was a crumpled paper tissue, thick with nasal mucus. There were large quantities of white blood cells (leukocytes—*see* Chapter 1, page 16), which were ideal for typing. Analysis confirmed that the same individual was responsible for Louise's death. Who was he?

Fortunately, the police had other clues to go on. On the carpet in the rear of Louise's car, examiners found a clear dusty shoe print with an unusual ribbed pattern on the sole. A number of dark blue fibers were trapped in the crevices of the rear seat's upholstery, and there was a peculiar pattern of pricked marks in the roof's fabric padding.

One police officer remarked that he had seen a similar pricked pattern somewhere before. It was the imprint of a type of security badge worn on a cap. Guessing that the blue fibers might have come from a guard's uniform, the police contacted local fabric manufacturers. Within two days, a company in the Bronx produced a match and named the three garment manufacturers in New York who had bought the fabric. The net was tightening on the unknown killer. A few days later, the police burglary unit reported that the shoe print in the car was identical with one found at the scene of a recent liquor store robbery. They had security video pictures from the hold-up and had been holding three suspects for questioning.

One was a Dudley Friar, age twenty-nine, who had a fifteen-year record of minor theft and violence. Friar worked at night as a hotel security guard. Investigators took nasal swabs from each suspect for DNA typing. Friar's sample matched, and the laboratory claimed that it was likely only six men in the United States would have exactly the same profile. Faced with all the evidence against him, Friar confessed. He was sentenced to three terms of life imprisonment.

A Woman Scorned?

Husband and wife Jim and Lisa Peng came from Taiwan to California, where Jim set up a company manufacturing CB radios. After the birth of their two children, Lisa returned to Taiwan, but the couple would often visit each other.

Jim, however, also had a girlfriend in California, named Jennifer Ji, and they had a son, Kevin. On August 18, 1993, Jim went to see Jennifer at her home in Mission Viejo, Orange County, and found a horrifying scene. His girlfriend lay in a huge pool of dried blood, and baby Kevin had been suffocated in his crib.

When the sheriff's officers arrived, Peng handed them a button he had found

An odontologist takes an impression of a suspect's teeth in dental wax. Although this may be to compare to a bite mark on a victim, enough saliva will be left on the impression for a later DNA analysis, if required.

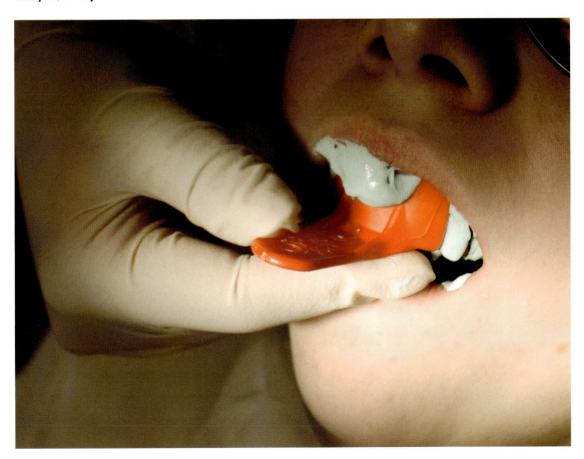

on the floor. It appeared to have fallen from a woman's dress—but not Jennifer's.

At first, investigators assumed this to be a typical case of sexual assault and murder. Jennifer had been stabbed eighteen times, and there was a clear bite wound on her left arm. However, samples taken from her body failed to establish that a sexual assault had taken place, and Jim Peng was considered a prime suspect of the murder.

Investigators then learned that Lisa, on a visit from Taiwan, was staying at Jim's home. Lisa agreed to let officers search for a dress with a missing button. They found nothing—but in the closet were two bags stuffed with dresses, underwear, and shoes, all slashed to pieces. With some embarrassment, Jim explained that these were Jennifer's. Some time back, his wife had arrived unexpectedly to find Jennifer living with him. In a violent rage, Lisa had destroyed all of Jennifer's clothes.

This alleged display of uncontrolled fury suggested that Lisa was a likely suspect in the two murders. An **odontologist** took a wax impression of her teeth. Although this closely matched photographs of the bite on Jennifer's arm, it was not in itself sufficient evidence to detain Lisa, who returned to Taiwan—before a sample of her blood could be taken.

Investigators used PCR to develop swabs of saliva taken from the bite, but the first test results merely narrowed the search to twenty people in 100. Saliva recovered from the wax impression produced the same result. This was a significant finding, but a probability of twenty in 100 was not enough to make a case. A second PCR test narrowed the probability to one in 100. Taking the two probabilities together, this gave a figure of twenty in 100 x 200—that is, one in 1,000.

There was enough DNA in the saliva from the bite mark for the forensic analysts to suggest carrying out a more accurate—but much slower— restriction fragment length polymorphism (RFLP) analysis. While this was being done, the investigators told Jim Peng that they could eliminate Lisa from the inquiry if she provided a sample of her blood. Lisa traveled again from Taiwan and, confident that there were no traces of her blood at the crime scene, she remained for more than a week in California with her husband. The RFLP tests provided a positive match, and on January 7, 1994, Lisa was arrested for both murders.

During the trial, Lisa's lawyers claimed that Jim Peng was the killer, and the jury could not reach a verdict. Lisa was convicted at a retrial and sentenced, in

PROCEDURE **MAIL ORDER PLAGUE**

The structure of DNA is fully understood, details of the human genome are available on the Internet to researchers, and a number of laboratories are even able to synthesize many DNA sequences on request. In 2006, a British investigative journalist approached one of these laboratories and asked if they could supply a specific sequence of DNA. They were happy to say they could. The journalist had requested a section of the anthrax virus. He has since pointed out that it would be possible to obtain another sequence, and for a third—illegal—laboratory to construct the actual virus. This is a very clear and present danger, and there is an urgent need for much closer supervision and control than at present.

Anthrax bacteria photographed under the microscope. The infection is almost always fatal. The "anthrax letters" in 2001, and the deaths that followed, provoked a major panic in the United States.

1995, to life imprisonment without possibility of parole. However, in a unanimous ruling by the appeal court in October 1999, the conviction was reversed, on the grounds that police had failed to advise Lisa of her rights, ignored her requests for a lawyer, demanded that she confess, and then used her husband as their agent to obtain incriminating statements.

The Trial of the Century

The trial of former football star O.J. Simpson, which opened on January 24, 1995, is now generally regarded as the trial of the century because it fascinated the public for so long.

On the night of June 12–13, 1994, a bloodstained dog was found wandering near the home of Nicole Brown Simpson, O.J.'s ex-wife, on Bundy Drive in the upscale district of Brentwood, Los Angeles. The dog led a neighbor to Nicole's body, lying in a pool of blood outside the door to her condominium. Nearby was the body of Ronald Goldman, a waiter at the restaurant where Nicole had earlier dined with her mother. He had come to return her mother's eyeglasses, which she had inadvertently left behind. Both had been savagely slashed to death.

Police detectives went immediately to Simpson's home on Rockingham Avenue, only a few miles away. His white Ford Bronco was outside, with a smear of blood on the door. A high wall surrounded the premises and the gate was locked. Concerned that there might be more victims, the police climbed over the wall. In the guest wing, they found Brian "Kato" Kaelin, who told them that Simpson had left earlier in a limo to catch a plane from the airport to Chicago. In the grounds, a detective found a bloodstained right-hand leather glove, which matched a left-hand glove later found at Bundy Drive. There was also a trail of blood drops leading to the front door of the house.

Back at the crime scene, investigators found bloody footprints leading to a rear gate. To the left of this trail there were five drops of blood that suggested the killer had injured his left hand. Officers collected samples, along with the blood of the victims.

When the police succeeded in contacting Simpson at his Chicago hotel, he agreed to return to Los Angeles by the earliest available flight. When he arrived, the middle finger of his left hand was bandaged. He gave several different explanations of how he had cut himself, and investigators took a full sample of

During the trial of O.J. Simpson, there was great controversy in court over the significance of DNA analysis. Among the evidence presented was a pair of bloodstained gloves discovered during the investigation of the murders.

his blood. Analysts later confirmed that the DNA from the blood drops at Bundy Drive matched Simpson's.

On June 14, 1994, many more bloodstains were found in his Bronco. On the carpet on the driver's side, a partial bloody shoe print contained Nicole Brown Simpson's DNA, and a stain on the center console yielded both Simpson's and Goldman's DNA. On the steering wheel, the instrument panel, and the driver's sidewall, the stains were of Simpson's blood. At his home, there were more drops of his blood in the entrance hallway and master bedroom. Investigators also picked up a pair of dark socks and bagged them as evidence, but they did not detect blood on them until later. This provoked controversy at the trial, and the accusation that the police had planted this evidence.

On June 17, 1994, the day after Nicole Brown Simpson's funeral, Simpson was notified that a warrant had been issued for his arrest on double murder charges. What followed—his flight in his Bronco, apparently on the way to Mexico—provided high drama for the TV-viewing public, but is not part of the DNA story.

Arguing the Evidence

By the time of the trial, Simpson had assembled a dream team for his defense. It included three leading attorneys—Robert Shapiro, Johnnie Cochran, and F. Lee Bailey—Harvard University Law Professor Alan Dershowitz, and Barry Scheck, founder of the Innocence Project (see Chapter 6, pages 82–83). Kary Mullis, the inventor of PCR, was named as a defense witness, but was not called to testify.

The prosecution, led by Assistant District Attorney Marcia Clark, was confident that the DNA evidence alone was enough to convict Simpson. Three separate laboratories—Cellmark, the California Department of Justice, and the Los Angeles Police Department—had performed a range of tests. RFLP analysis of the blood drops beside the footprints yielded a one in 170 million match with that of Simpson. PCR testing gave a one in 240,000 match on four footprints,

▷ **The trail of bloody shoe prints on the pathway leading to the door of Nicole Brown Simpson's condominium. It was established that these had been made by a pair of Bruno Magli shoes, which O.J. Simpson denied possessing.**

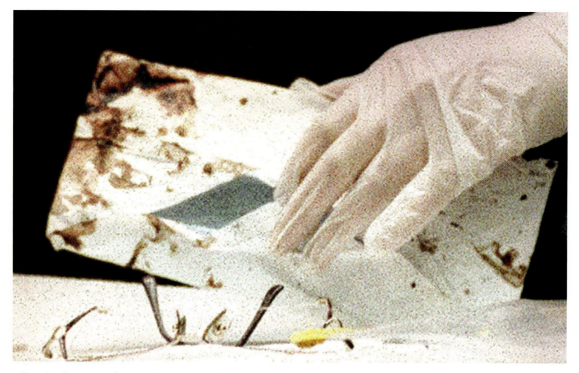

When he became the unwitting second victim of the Simpson murders, Ronald Goldman had been returning a pair of eyeglasses that Nicole's mother had left in the restaurant where he worked.

and a one in 5,200 on a fifth footprint. The defense argued that the blood samples could have become so degraded that the analyses were invalid. However, Harlan Levy, a legal expert on DNA, has pointed out, in the book *Postmortem* (1996):

> *Degradation would have had to have been so severe that the DNA disappeared in each of five separate blood drops. Next, a transfer would have had to have taken place in which the blood present in Simpson's blood sample made its way into each of the blood drops themselves. Finally, there would have had to have been a failure in five separate controls, each designed to determine whether contamination had taken place.*

Ultimately, the prosecution had great difficulty in presenting the evidence, and holding the jury's attention. In the end, the prosecution failed, and Simpson was found not guilty on October 3, 1995. The Brown and Goldman families then brought a civil suit against him for the two murders. They were in a better legal position than the Los Angeles prosecutors because a civil trial calls only for proof by weight of evidence, rather than proof beyond reasonable doubt, as in a criminal case. Also, the jury's verdict did not have to be unanimous. At the criminal trial, much had been made of the fact that the bloody footprints had been produced by a distinctive pair of size twelve Bruno Magli shoes, which Simpson denied ever having owned. At the civil trial, however, the prosecution produced a number of photographs showing him wearing a pair.

On February 4, 1997, the jury unanimously found Simpson responsible for the deaths of Nicole Brown Simpson and Ronald Goldman.

Christopher Darden, director of prosecutions for the Los Angeles jurisdiction, at the 1995 murder trial of O.J. Simpson.

chapter 6

Questions of the Law

DNA evidence has been questioned by the defense in a number of cases. On the other hand, more than 100 convicted persons have later been exonerated.

L ike fingerprinting two generations earlier, DNA profiling took some years—and several pioneer cases—before it could be accepted as evidence before the courts. In the United States, one of the problems is that not all states apply exactly the same standards to scientific testimony. Also, some prosecuting attorneys did make excessive claims about DNA's potential for identifying an individual, which delayed its acceptance for some time.

The first precedent to be considered was the Frye Standard, named after the 1923 case of *Frye v. United States*. In this case, the defense wanted to prevent polygraph, or lie detector, evidence being presented in court. The District of Columbia trial court granted the motion to exclude it, and the D.C. Appellate Court upheld its decision. The court ruled on the grounds that polygraph evidence, which used technology

◁ **Federal Judge William Steele Sessions was appointed director of the FBI in July 1987. He was responsible for large-scale reorganization within the Bureau. However, he was accused of allowing his wife to violate regulations, and was fired by President Clinton in 1993.**

developed just two years earlier, had not yet gained general acceptance. Gradually, all U.S. states accepted the Frye Standard and it served as the check on all scientific and technological evidence for fifty years. However, with the increasing development in scientific research, the U.S. Supreme Court drew up a new set of Federal Rules of Evidence in 1975, and these were confirmed in Congress. These rules were designed to give greater powers of discretion to individual judges. Then, in 1993, the Supreme Court introduced a new standard, the Daubert Standard, named after the case of *Daubert v. Merrell Dow Pharmaceuticals*.

The Daubert rules were intended to give judges even more freedom than they had under the Federal Rules. Not all states have adopted the Daubert Standard, and reports of pre-trial hearings often refer to either a Frye motion or a Daubert motion, usually entered by the defense. When DNA evidence was still new, this happened often. Today, such a motion is generally seen as nothing more than a delaying tactic by the defense.

In court, O.J. Simpson is shown autorads comparing DNA profiles of the various samples of blood obtained from the crime scene and the interior of his Bronco. The jury found the evidence difficult to understand.

KEY FACTS **THE DAUBERT STANDARD**

- The theory or technique must have been scientifically tested.
- Qualified scientific experts—other than those scientists who developed the theory or technique—must review it and publish their findings in recognized scientific journals. (This is known as "peer review.")
- Information about the theory or technique's error rate, and its potential for error, must be made clear.
- Those responsible for carrying out any tests or operations—for example, a polygraph test—must do so according to strict standards.
- The scientific community must have widely accepted the theory or technique.

DNA Evidence Rejected

In 1987, restriction fragment length polymorphism (RFLP) evidence (*see* Chapter 3, page 35) was accepted in Florida in the retrial of Tommy Lee Andrews (*see* Chapter 3, page 37). In the same year, a notable case was heard in a New York State court. Joseph Castro was accused of stabbing Vilma Ponce and her young daughter to death. A commercial laboratory that had only just taken up forensic work subjected a single spot of blood—allegedly Vilma Ponce's—found on Castro's watch to DNA analysis.

Autorads (*see* Chapter 3, page 35) were produced in court, but they were not of good quality. Remarkably, after they had testified, four of the expert witnesses, for both the prosecution and the defense, met together and advised the court that the scientific evidence was inadequate. The judge ruled that the RFLP identification of Ponce's blood could not be admitted. He did, however, allow evidence that the blood on the watch was not Castro's. He also remarked that only two people in the courtroom knew whether the blood was Vilma Ponce's: the laboratory analyst and the accused himself. Joseph Castro was convicted on other evidence, and later confessed to the murder.

To take a sample of trace evidence at a crime scene, a cotton swab is slightly moistened with distilled water.

In the published judgment, determining whether RFLP evidence could be accepted in court, the court outlined three questions that extended the Frye Standard:

- Is there a sound theory behind DNA testing?
- Are the techniques for testing able to give reliable results?
- Were the tests performed properly in this case?

The reliability of DNA analysis, in general, was recognized, but the third question was certainly not established in this particular case.

The Problem of Population Statistics

In 1990, the Federal Bureau of Investigation (FBI) accepted RFLP analysis as evidence for the first time. On the evening of February 27, 1988, David Hartlaub's body, shot at least six times, was found dumped outside a bank in Perkins Township, Ohio. Hell's Angels had shot him at another location—by mistake in a killing for hire—and there were no witnesses. Someone, however, had driven his van to the spot where his corpse was dumped.

There was fresh blood inside the van, which was not Hartlaub's. When the gang was rounded up, the blood showed the same genetic pattern as one of the members, John Ray Bonds. He was charged with the murder and brought to trial in a federal—not a state—court.

The defense mounted a fierce attack on DNA evidence in general, and on the

PROCEDURE   EVIDENCE ABROAD

In British courts, and courts that follow British principles, the judge decides whether evidence can be accepted or not. If it is accepted, it establishes an example that is followed in future cases, unless overruled by a higher court. In Britain, on rare occasions, the House of Lords will listen to appeals on a point of law, if it is thought to be of public importance. The House of Lords is the final court of judicial appeal, and is equivalent to the U.S. Supreme Court.

In many other countries, an examining magistrate considers most cases and decides whether there is enough evidence—and what that evidence should be—to go to trial. Generally, the court's decision can later be appealed in a higher court.

FBI analysis in particular. The defense claimed that it failed to take into account the possibility of local variations in population genetic percentages (*see* Chapter 3, pages 44–45). However, the judge ruled in favor of the prosecution and allowed the DNA evidence. In the same year, in another case, a federal appellate (appeals) court upheld the admissibility of RFLP evidence.

In 1991, Linda Axell was accused—also in a federal court—of killing the owner of a convenience store. Several strands of her hair, with scraps of tissue attached, were found in the victim's fingers, and were enough for RFLP analysis. An unusual hearing on admissibility was held, involving testimony from many experts from all over the country. The inquiry took a long time but, eventually, the judge allowed the DNA evidence, including the statistical calculations.

Unfortunately, in December 1991, a controversy over the use of generalized population statistics broke out in the pages of the leading journal *Science*. This had an immediate effect on two cases heard in 1992 in the Alameda County Supreme Court, California. In both cases, the court ruled the admissibility of RFLP evidence. However, the appellate court, in the light of the raging controversy, excluded the use of DNA evidence until the controversy was resolved. It was not until 1994 that calculations of frequency were ruled admissible.

PCR-STR Admissibility

Polymerase chain reaction (PCR) analysis (*see* Chapter 3, page 43) had already been accepted in many trial courts for nearly ten years. This was because, in the early cases, PCR was quite a simple system. This situation gradually changed, however, as more sophisticated short tandem repeat (STR) systems (*see* Chapter 3, page 43) were developed. Along the way, many people have questioned the reliability of the PCR method itself, and challenged the expertise of the analysts using it. Some of the commercial organizations manufacturing PCR systems have been unwilling to provide specific scientific details. Also, as the systems have not been peer reviewed, they fail the Daubert Standard. Consequently, several states have refused to accept PCR-STR evidence since 1999.

Helping the Wrongly Convicted

DNA evidence has, however, proved very valuable in freeing men wrongly imprisoned for assault. In the spring and summer of 1987, two women in the San Francisco Bay Area were abducted and raped. The victims' descriptions of the assailant, and his method, led the police to believe that the same man was responsible. One woman identified a suspect from a photograph, and later identified the same man at an identity parade lineup and at a preliminary hearing. The arrested man requested a forensic DNA test to establish his innocence and the prosecution agreed to his request. Dr. Edward Blake, who had been working with the Cetus Corporation on the development of the DNA analysis system, undertook the test. He showed that the defendant was not connected with the assaults.

Two years later, police arrested Armando Quintanilla for attempted rape, close to the scene of the first crime. He so closely resembled the first suspect that detectives asked Dr. Blake for another analysis. The results showed that Quintanilla had a type of DNA that occurs in less than 10 percent of the population. With this, and other circumstantial evidence, he was convicted of a number of felonies and sentenced to ninety-nine years, plus life.

The Innocence Project

In the early 1990s, lawyer Barry Scheck, who had been a member of the defense team in the case of Joseph Castro, became concerned that innocent people were serving time in prison. He was convinced that DNA typing could prove it. With the approval of the National Association of Criminal Defense, he and his colleague Peter Neufeld set up a DNA taskforce, which became known as the Innocence Project. They were inspired by the case of Gary Dotson.

In 1977, in Illinois, Dotson was accused of attacking Cathleen Webb. He was

Jubilation on every face, as Larry Fuller, escorted by his attorneys, leaves a Crowley, Texas, courthouse in October 2006. Convicted of rape in 1981, Fuller—a decorated Vietnam vet—served half of a 50-year sentence before DNA analysis exonerated him.

convicted in 1979, mainly because of Webb's eyewitness identification. Eight years later, she withdrew her identification of Dotson, and in 1988 DNA typing showed that he was innocent. However, the judge would not accept either the DNA evidence or Webb's withdrawal of her evidence, and refused to release Dotson, who had spent nearly twelve years in prison. In the end, the state governor granted Dotson clemency—although he was not officially pardoned.

As a professor in the Cardozo School of Law at Yeshiva University, New York City, Scheck invited lawyers to contact him with cases they believed to be wrongful convictions. He and Neufeld offered their services unpaid where DNA typing could be used to reverse a conviction. At first, Scheck received few applications until, in 1992, he appeared on TV's *Phil Donahue Show*. He appealed publicly for anyone who believed that they, or a member of their family, had been wrongly convicted to contact the Innocence Project.

The letters began to pour in, most cases dating from a time before DNA typing came into use. To date, the Innocence Project has already proved that more than

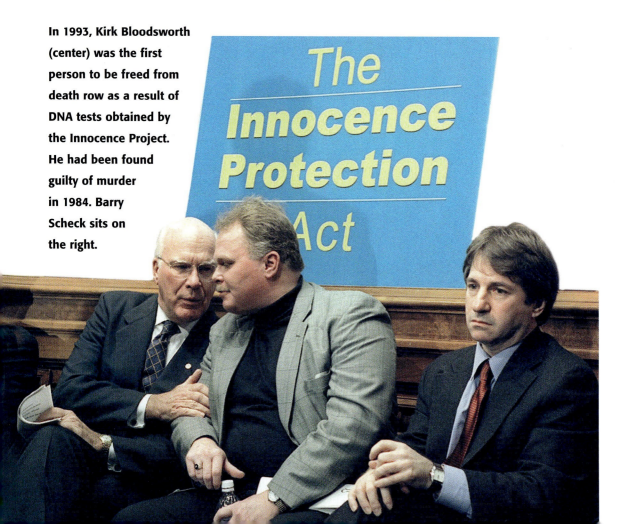

In 1993, Kirk Bloodsworth (center) was the first person to be freed from death row as a result of DNA tests obtained by the Innocence Project. He had been found guilty of murder in 1984. Barry Scheck sits on the right.

The Innocence Protection Act

CASE STUDY MISTAKEN IDENTITY

An important case occurred in England in 1999. DNA evidence was recovered from the scene of a burglary in the Manchester area. Using the national database, investigators detected a match of six loci (*see* Chapter 3, page 34) with a blood sample taken from a man arrested for hitting his daughter in an earlier domestic dispute. In spite of the fact that he lived 200 miles (320 kilometers) from Manchester, had advanced Parkinson's disease, could hardly dress himself, and could not drive a car, the police insisted that the DNA match was positive proof. Experts for the prosecution testified that the chance that the match was incorrect was one in 37 million, and the man was convicted.

After the man had been in prison for several months, his lawyer succeeded in demanding a more accurate test. A new analysis was performed, using ten loci instead of six. There was no match at the additional four loci, showing the prisoner to be innocent.

The statistical calculation, based solely on six loci, does not mean that investigators cannot match more than one individual in 37 million. It means that—*on average*—they may have to search 37 million before a single match is found. In fact, population geneticists have pointed out that it is possible to obtain a six-loci match in dozens of individuals from a databank of some 700,000.

180 people spent an average ten years in prison—one man had served twenty-three years—for crimes they did not commit. The project's work continues. Jane Siegel Greene, executive director of the project for many years, once said:

DNA is not the magic bullet. It is not going to fix the criminal justice system, but what it does do is open this window on what is wrong with the system. It allows us to show with absolute certainty that these people are truly innocent.

In Washington, D.C., the Armed Forces Pathology Institute maintains a repository of the DNA—mainly as oral samples—of all active service personnel, together with that of civilians who are employed in a military establishment.

Since the setting-up of the Cardozo Innocence Project, similar projects have been established in nearly every state in the United States, many of them by university law departments.

DNA Databanks

With the help of computer technology, it was easy to set up databanks to compare DNA from a new crime. In 1989, the state of Virginia was the first in the United States to establish such a databank. It was made up of profiles from blood samples from convicted felons and a number of unsolved crime scenes across the state.

In the summer of 1994, the body of Hope Denise Hall was discovered in her Petersburg apartment. She had been attacked. The only suspect was cleared when his DNA did not match samples from the crime scene, and for two years the crime remained unsolved. Then, in 1996, the Virginia operatives made a historic cold hit—matching the samples with the DNA of Shermaine Ali Johnson, who was already serving a 100-year sentence for multiple crimes. After a sensational trial, he was sentenced to death.

Following the passing of the DNA Identification Act in 1994, many local and state databanks were established in the United States. By 1998, all fifty states had passed laws requiring local police departments to take DNA samples. However, each state is individually responsible for enacting legislation, and the 1994 Act limits the use of databanks to the recording of convicted criminals. As a result, there is no consistency in the types of offenses that require the police to collect a DNA sample.

Every state records the DNA of sex offenders, but individual states vary in whether they take DNA samples from convicted murderers, burglars, and those who commit crimes against juveniles. Some go further, taking DNA samples from all arrested suspects.

Also in 1994, in an attempt to coordinate DNA records nationally, the Federal Bureau of Investigation (FBI) also set up the Combined DNA Index System (CODIS). All fifty states contribute to CODIS. The databank consists of STR profiles (*see* Chapter 3, page 43), and two types of record. First, there are convicted offender profiles, which include fifteen STRs. Second, the FBI also collects profiles from unsolved crimes—forensic unknowns—consisting of ten STRs.

KEY FACTS ENGLISH NATIONAL DATA BASE

The FBI CODIS is the second largest in the world, but the largest is the National DNA Database (NDNADB) of England and Wales, which was set up in 1995. Scotland maintains a separate—but linked—system. Although RFLP remains the final means of positive identification in the UK, the database also records STR profiles as a second generation multiplex (SGM). This identifies seven loci, and forensic scientists claim the method can identify one person in 50 million—nearly the total population of England and Wales. The system is run by the Forensic Science Service and now holds the profiles of more than 3.5 million people.

Initially, under the Police and Criminal Evidence Act (PACE) of 1984, police could take DNA samples only from anyone suspected of having committed a serious arrestable offense. The Act also stipulated that when "a person is not suspected of having committed an offense or is not prosecuted or is acquitted of the offense, the sample must be destroyed." A 1994 Act allowed police to take samples in a wider range of circumstances. The 1994 Act also stated that if a person was found innocent, the samples (including fingerprints) should be destroyed.

However, the Criminal Justice and Police Act of 2001 allowed samples to be kept indefinitely when they were taken "in connection with the investigation of an offense"—and this included those "investigated" but considered innocent. An appeal against this provision was taken right up to the House of Lords—the final court of appeal. The House of Lords dismissed the appeal—declaring that the records did not intrude unacceptably upon personal privacy.

In March 2006, a fine point of British law was established. A schoolteacher was accused of assault and taken into custody. Police decided not to press charges—and then took her fingerprints and a DNA sample. The High Court ruled that she should have been released immediately, that the samples were taken "without appropriate authority," and should be destroyed.

A researcher at the National Institute of Health, preparing samples for DNA analysis.

Investigators had an early success when they linked a man convicted of sexual assault in Orlando, Florida, in 1993 to another assault that took place in the same state, in 1991. By the end of 2005, CODIS had accumulated 2.8 million offender profiles and 124,200 forensic profiles, and produced more than 27,700 matches.

In 2004, California ruled that all suspects arrested for a crime—as well as individuals convicted of misdemeanors—should have their DNA recorded. The state databank is now the third largest in the world.

Other National Databases

The Canadian National DNA Databank (NDDB) did not begin operation until 2000, but already it has scored some notable successes. By early 2006, the NDDB had provided matches in approximately 5,000 cases, ranging from simple break-and-enter crimes to very complex high-profile murder and physical assault investigations.

Some of these were cold cases more than twenty years old. At present, the samples held by the NDDB are from convicted persons. Similar databanks are being gradually built up in Australia and New Zealand.

Across the world, most developed nations now have national databases. A recent Interpol (International Criminal Police Organization) survey reported that the law enforcement agencies of seventy-seven of its member states currently carried out DNA analysis, and that more than forty of these had set up national databases.

An International Databank

The UK already shares its DNA database with a number of other countries. As with fingerprints, there is clearly a potential value in the establishment of a worldwide database. However, for practical purposes, it would probably have to be restricted to cases of murder and sex crimes. In 2000, such international collaboration could have caught up quickly with John Eric Armstrong, age twenty-six, a crewman aboard USS *Nimitz*. He was involved in the killings of at least sixteen prostitutes, over a period of eight years, at ports around the world.

There are huge practical difficulties with setting up an international database of this kind. The first big problem is the huge amount of data investigators would have to search through. Without doubt, an enormous backlog would build up. Also, the more samples entered into the system, the greater likelihood of false matches. To counter this, investigators would have to record a greater number of loci, which would take more time. Older records might not be compatible with more recent ones. To complicate matters further, different countries do not all employ the same analytical standards, or have the same legislation regarding the taking of DNA samples.

In addition, an international database would present certain difficulties in the interpretation of population statistics. Prosecuting attorneys would find their arguments constantly under attack by the defense. Juries could become even more confused and quickly lose faith in DNA identification.

The Rights of the Individual

DNA profiling is an attractive technique for law enforcement, and has wide applications in the fight against crime. It is therefore very tempting, as current English law shows, to broaden the conditions that allow the authorities to take samples and keep records on file. Civil liberties organizations have protested vigorously, but with little success. Even Germany, which for many years imposed very strict limitations on the taking and storing of DNA samples, has now relaxed the restrictions so far that one critic has described the latest change in the law as a step towards genetic registration. With the growing demand for **biometric** identity cards, it seems very likely that DNA profiles will eventually be demanded of every member of the population in every developed country.

While law enforcement agencies can justly claim the importance of profiling, there is another area where genetic information could be subject to abuse. An individual's gene structure could indicate the possibility of that person developing a fatal or debilitating disease. If employers or insurers obtained that information, it could be very damaging for that person.

There are specific genes, also, for racial type. Critics have protested that this can be discriminatory, and the police have been cautious about the use of this kind of analysis. There have been cases, however, in which a laboratory has provided essential information. For example: in March 2003, Louisiana police were working on a case of serial killing, and looking for a white man who had been seen lurking near one of the crime scenes. However, the commercial laboratory DNAPrint Genomics assured them that the killer was 85 percent sub-Saharan African, and 15 percent Native American. An African-American man, called in for questioning about two unrelated murders, was found to have matching DNA.

There is, finally, the question of how, and when, a sample may be obtained from an individual. In some countries, it is mandatory, like the taking of fingerprints. In others, it must be voluntary, if it is done before conviction. The taking of blood and other intimate fluids is invasive. The English police got around this by declaring that hairs and cells swabbed from the inside of the mouth were non-intimate, and could be taken without the individual's permission. DNA analysis has come far in just twenty years. The pioneers who made it possible cannot have imagined how rapidly it would develop. Who knows what the next twenty years will bring?

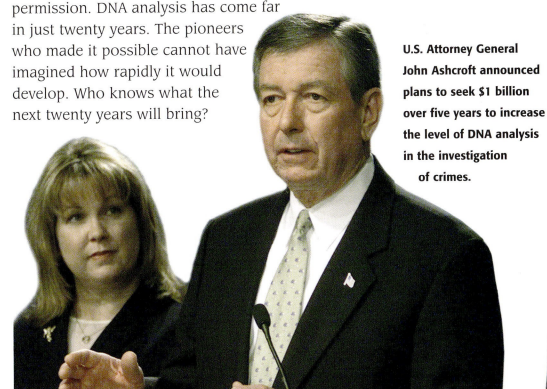

U.S. Attorney General John Ashcroft announced plans to seek $1 billion over five years to increase the level of DNA analysis in the investigation of crimes.

Glossary

agglutination sticking or clumping together

amplified term used to describe the multiplication of DNA strands by polymerase chain reaction (PCR)

anatomists scientists who study the physical structure of the body

autoradiograph image produced on x-ray film by radioactive "probes" attached to DNA fragments

biohazard the danger of contracting disease by contact with infected traces

biometric employing various physical attributes, such as body measurement, fingerprints, or images of the iris of the eye

chromosomes the twenty-three pairs of bodies in the nucleus that determine all the hereditary characteristics

degrade to break down into smaller molecules

deoxyribonucleic acid DNA, the molecule found in the cell nucleus that contains all the genes

electrophoresis an analytic process that separates molecules by their size

enzymes chemicals related to proteins; they are catalysts—causing chemical reactions without themselves being changed—and control all the metabolism that takes place in the body

epithelial describing layers of cells that cover the surfaces of the body

geneticists scientists who study the genes that determine hereditary characteristics

helixes a form that goes round and round, and up, and up, without a change in diameter; a so-called "spiral" staircase is strictly a helix

hemoglobin the colored content of red blood cells, responsible for carrying oxygen throughout the body

hepatitis an infection of the liver

heredity the sum of qualities and characteristics inherited from ancestors

HIV human immunodeficiency virus—the virus that is the cause of AIDS (acquired immune deficiency syndrome)

hydrogen peroxide a liquid that contains one more atom of oxygen than water; it is generally used as a solution in water

locus a word from the Latin (plural loci) meaning place; a point on the DNA chain where it can be fragmented

metabolism the chemical processes that go on in the body to provide energy and maintain life

mitochondria small round bodies in the cell, outside the nucleus, which contain a form of DNA known as mtDNA. This comes only from the mother, and is transmitted unchanged through the female line

molecules chemical compounds made up of two or more atoms

nucleic acid chemical compound that can be isolated from the nucleus; there are two types of nucleic acid—DNA and RNA; DNA contains less oxygen than RNA

nucleotides the "building blocks" of DNA and RNA

nucleus mass found in the center of every cell—with the exception of red blood cells—that contains DNA

odontologist a dental surgeon, with experience of the shape of the bite

ovum the female reproductive cell, which is fertilized by the male sperm to start conception

pathologist a scientist, usually one who works with the medical examiner to analyze all the evidence obtained from a dead body at autopsy, or, in other fields, one who studies diseases

phenolphthalein a dye that is colorless, but turns pink in the presence of acid

phosphorus chemical element, symbol P, which exists in several forms; it is an essential element for living organisms

physiologist a scientist who studies the vital processes in living animals and plants

precipitin a cloudy substance produced when serum from two different sources is mixed together

proteins a very large group of compounds that are an essential part of the animal diet. Proteins are necessary components of many parts of all animal and plant bodies

purine bases five nitrogen-containing compounds—adenine (A), cytosine (C), guanine (G), thymine (T), and uracil (U); the "rungs" of the DNA ladder are made up of A, C, G, and T; RNA contains A, C, G, and U

radioactive giving out alpha particles, electrons, and gamma-radiation (very short wavelength x-rays)

ribose a relatively simple sugar-like compound that contains five carbon atoms; glucose contains six

RNA ribonucleic acid, which is concerned with the synthesis of proteins in the cell

serologists scientists who study and analyze body fluids

short tandem repeats repeating sequences of identical, or similar, DNA, between two and five units long

thermal cycler equipment used in the amplification of DNA by polymerase chain reaction (PCR)

variable number tandem repeats (VNTR) repeating units of identical, or similar, DNA, which occur one after the other in a particular region of a chromosome; the number of repeated units varies between individuals

Learn More About

A wealth of information on DNA and body evidence, as well as a broader look at forensic science, is available from the various media. Listed below are books and Web sites that link to government bureaus, professional bodies, reports, magazine and newspaper articles, and other sources.

Books

Buckleton, John S., Christopher M. Triggs, and Simon J. Walsh. *Forensic DNA Evidence Interpretation*. Boca Raton, FL: CRC Press, 2004.

Connors, Edward, et al. *Convicted by Juries, Exonerated by Science*. Washington, DC: U.S. Department of Justice, 1996.

Committee on DNA Technology in Forensic Science, National Research Council. *DNA Technology in Forensic Science*. Washington: National Academy Press, 1992.

Lee, Henry, and Frank Timady. *Blood Evidence*. Philadelphia: Perseus Books, 2003.

Levine, Louis, Henrietta Margolis Nunno, and Lawrence Kobilinsky. *Forensic DNA Analysis*. New York: Chelsea House, 2006.

Maples, William R. *Dead Men Do Tell Tales*. New York: Doubleday, 1994.

Nickell, Joe, and John F. Fischer. *Crime Science*. Lexington: University Press of Kentucky, 1999.

Ragle, Larry. *Crime Scene*. New York: Avon Books, 2002.

Rudin, Norah, and Keith Inman. *Forensic DNA Analysis, 2nd edition*. Boca Raton, FL: CRC Press, 2002.

Saferstein, Richard (ed). *Forensic Science Handbook*. Englewood Cliffs, NJ: Prentice-Hall, 1982.

Watson, James D., and Andrew Berry. *DNA: The Secret of Life*. New York: Knopf, 2003.

Web Sites

Innocence Project: www.innocenceproject.org

Scientific Testimony: An Online Journal: www.scientific.org/tutorials/articles/riley/riley.html

Who Dunnit?: www.cyberbee.com/whodunnit/crime.html

About the Author

Brian Innes began his professional career as a research biochemist in industry. He later transferred to chemical journalism, and was subsequently creative director and deputy chairman of Orbis Publishing, a leading London publisher. His first book on a criminal subject, *The Book of Outlaws*, was published in 1966.

Since 1990 he has concentrated on forensic science, beginning with a succession of articles for the weekly magazine *Real Life Crimes*. His more recent books include *Bodies of Evidence, Profile of a Criminal Mind, Body in Question,* and *Serial Killers*. He is a member of the Crime Writers' Association, and chairman of the panel of judges for their Gold Dagger award for non-fiction writing. He currently lives in the south of France.

Quoted Sources

p. 22—*Real Life Crimes* (London, 1993), issue 14, p.313

p. 50—*What Every Law Enforcement Officer Should Know About DNA Evidence* (1999), booklet published by the National Institute of Justice

p. 62—*The Encyclopedia of Serial Killers* (Checkmark Books, New York, 2000), by Michael Newton

p. 74—*Postmortem: The O. J. Simpson Case* (New York, Basic Books, 1996), ed. Jeffrey Adamson

p. 85—Jane Siegel Greene on www.innocenceproject.org

p. 88—www.ojp.usdoj.gov/nij/topics/forensics/events/dnasummit

Index